C000091972

Contents

Introduction

Projects typically originate from identified problems or opportunities. The aim is to ensure project success, benefiting both organizations and project managers. This book delves into project management by using a case study to explore successful project management strategies. It covers project initiation, planning, execution, monitoring, and closure.

Your success as a project manager hinges on your ability to identify and address ethical concerns, especially as your projects grow in complexity. Ethical conduct is a vital requirement for maintaining good standing with the Project Management Institute (PMI) and holding their certifications. However, ethical decision-making can be challenging due to conflicts of interest, fear of failure, and business pressures. To excel, you must recognize your own ethical principles and apply them to your project's unique demands. This book aims to help you understand PMI's mandatory and aspirational ethical standards and incorporate the cultural expectations of your work environment into your daily decision-making. Ultimately, the goal is to uphold your personal integrity, maintain ethical project management, and enhance your business's ethical stance.

Many professionals become anxious when they hear the term "project requirements," but I don't, and you shouldn't either because we handle project requirements daily. Think about planning dinner with friends; you must coordinate schedules, food preferences, restaurant choices, and reservations to avoid dinner plans going awry. This illustrates managing project requirements, which is essentially determining what the business needs and setting project goals. Success requires thoroughness and consistency. We'll begin by discussing the benefits of good requirements and then proceed with a 10-step process for managing project requirements.

Project scheduling is a complex task that requires flexibility and skill. The goal is to complete the project within scope, on time, and within budget. We'll cover everything from creating a schedule management plan to developing, fine-tuning, and problem-solving for your project schedule. You'll also learn scheduling best practices. It's helpful to have some familiarity with project management concepts and terminology. Projects are unique endeavors with specific goals, a definite start and end, and often a budget. Key factors for project success include scope, time, cost, resources, and quality. We'll focus on scheduling concepts and techniques without tying them to a specific scheduling tool. We'll use a sample project, publishing a training guide and companion website, to demonstrate scheduling principles. This project has set deadlines, resource constraints, and deliverables, making it a practical example to explore. You'll learn how to build realistic schedules and manage them effectively, which you can apply to your own projects. Let's dive into the world of project scheduling and develop the skills you need to manage projects successfully.

Project managers have one primary job: delivering business value. Without providing value, running a project serves no purpose. Early in the project, you'll make adjustments as you assess the accuracy of your estimates. Your budget must adapt to factors such as emerging risks, actual purchase costs, stakeholder requests, evolving business needs, and errors in project deliverables. It's a dynamic environment, and adjusting project costs for accuracy is crucial to bolster stakeholder confidence. Therefore, I'll provide guidance not only on constructing your budget but also on adapting it as more information becomes available.

Psychologist Abraham Maslow once compared having only one tool to a hammer, making every problem look like a nail. As project managers, our role involves motivating and fostering effective teamwork, which can be quite challenging. To navigate these complexities, we need a variety of tools at our disposal. While I'm not a psychologist or sociologist, I can introduce you to some psychological and sociological frameworks that can be valuable for managing project teams. The aim of this book is to provide a practical overview of these frameworks, helping you understand their potential usefulness. With this knowledge, you can explore further as needed. Ultimately, this book will empower you to become a better leader, a more skilled communicator, and a successful project manager.

Project managers are primarily involved in communication. Effective communication is vital for successful projects, while poor communication is often blamed for problems. In today's fast-paced projects, numerous groups demand information, leading to email and voicemail overload. This book aims to help you streamline your communication process, offering strategies for prioritization and audience targeting. You'll learn how to create a communication plan to set expectations and produce clear, reader-friendly reports. We'll discuss common communication challenges. Mastering both the science and art of communication is essential for project managers.

Chapter 1 Project Management Foundations

What is a project?

Before diving into project management, let's clarify what a project is. A project is a time-limited effort with a distinct objective and typically a financial allocation. Unlike ongoing operations, projects have a clear start and finish. For example, implementing a new system is a project, completed when it's operational. The project's goal is to produce a unique outcome, such as enhancing scheduling in our hospital case study. Projects also come with budgets, which may include financial and resource constraints. Unlike routine operational tasks, projects have specific goals, budgets, and finite timelines. Reflecting on recent months, consider projects you've been involved in by evaluating their timeframes, distinctiveness, and resource allocations.

What is project management?

Project management goes beyond just organizing tasks and overseeing others; it's about applying knowledge, skills, tools, and techniques to achieve project objectives. It involves addressing key questions:

1. What problem or objective does the project aim to solve or achieve?

2. How will you approach and resolve this problem or seize the opportunity?

3. What's your detailed plan, including tasks, timelines, resources, and costs?

4. How will you determine when the project is successfully completed?

5. How did the project perform, and what lessons can be learned for future endeavors?

These questions encapsulate the essence of effective project management.

What it takes to be a project manager

Project managers are often perceived as highly organized individuals who excel at task execution. However, successful project management requires a diverse skill set and knowledge base:

1. Technical Skills: These include creating project plans, refining schedules, interpreting Gantt charts, utilizing the critical path method, and measuring performance.

2. Business Acumen: Project managers must grasp their organization's objectives, operations, and priorities to ensure their projects deliver value and align with the overall business strategy.

3. Problem Solving: Projects rarely go as planned, necessitating the ability to adapt, troubleshoot, and find solutions to keep the project on track.

4. Interpersonal Skills: Collaboration is key, as projects often involve individuals from various backgrounds and departments. Project managers must lead, foster teamwork, and facilitate effective communication.

5. Leadership: Exceptional project managers inspire and guide their teams, promote accountability, and motivate team members to excel.

The waterfall project management lifecycle

The traditional, or Waterfall, project management life cycle consists of five stages that guide a project from initiation to closure.

1. Initiating: This stage involves defining the project's purpose, scope, resource estimates, and costs, as well as identifying stakeholders and gaining their approval to proceed.

2. Planning: Here, a specialized team details the project's actions, methods, and completion criteria. Approval is sought before launching the project.

3. Executing: The project is officially launched, resources are onboarded, and work begins according to the plan.

4. Monitoring and Controlling: Continuous oversight of project progress occurs throughout most of the project, with corrective actions taken if it veers off the goal.

5. Closing: This final step involves client approval, performance documentation, gathering lessons learned, concluding contracts, and transitioning resources.

Waterfall project management is effective when goals, solutions, scope, and deliverables are well-defined, making it suitable for straightforward projects with little uncertainty and teams experienced in similar endeavors.

The agile project management lifecycle

Many modern projects require an adaptive approach, such as Agile. In Agile, teams work in Sprints to deliver production-quality, partial features at regular intervals, allowing for earlier value delivery and customer feedback to enhance the overall solution. Agile projects demand increased customer involvement and rely on smaller, experienced teams that work with minimal supervision.

The Agile life cycle, based on Jim Highsmith's 'Agile Project Management,' starts with envisioning, akin to Waterfall's initiation, where the product vision and initial goals are outlined, although these goals may evolve as the project progresses.

Speculate involves continuous feature list revision, prioritization, effort estimation, and risk identification.

During explore, independent, skilled teams build and deliver Sprint features. Adapt, or retrospective, is where feedback informs process adjustments and potential feature rework.

This cycle repeats for each Sprint until project completion, followed by a closing phase to document lessons learned. Agile is suited for projects where the solution evolves over time.

How organizational structure affects projects

Organizations vary in structure, impacting project execution. The functional hierarchy, where employees report to a single supervisor, prioritizes regular operations, making project success challenging due to limited project manager authority, resource allocation difficulties, and divided focus.

Matrix organizations, a modified hierarchy, offer weak, balanced, or strong support for projects, granting project managers some decision-making power. Resources report to both functional and project managers.

Projectized organizations prioritize projects, streamlining project manager authority, resource allocation, and project-focused staff. Project managers have significant autonomy. Understanding your organization's structure is crucial for project management.

How organizational culture affects projects

Organizational culture encompasses shared values, beliefs, assumptions, habits, and language guiding behaviors and decisions within an organization. It significantly impacts projects:

1. Alignment with Mission and Vision: Projects supporting the organization's mission receive more attention and resources, aiding decision-making.

2. Leadership and Authority: Clear goal setting and delegated responsibility enhance project outcomes, while limited authority necessitates collaboration with management.

3. Work Environment: Positive environments promote motivation and knowledge sharing. Negative ones may require more team management.

4. Rule Orientation: Cultures vary in adherence to rules versus nurturing innovation. Project managers should navigate rule-breaking judiciously.

5. Results vs. Procedures: Cultural norms dictate whether achieving objectives outweighs following procedures, impacting project boundaries.

6. Change Management: Risk-averse cultures require rigorous change processes, while adaptable cultures streamline change management.

7. Team Cultural Diversity: Cultural differences among team members influence reactions, communication, and team dynamics.

Project managers must consider and manage cultural factors to enhance project success.

Project management software options

Project managers can benefit from various software tools to simplify their tasks. These tools include:

1. Scheduling Software: Tools like Microsoft Project, Oracle Primavera, Jira, and more help build and manage project schedules. Ensure they align with your project management approach.

2. Word Processing: Essential for creating project documents, templates can streamline document creation.

3. Spreadsheet Program: Necessary for calculations, financial analysis, and risk assessment.

4. Presentation Software: Useful for conveying high-level project information and incorporating data from various documents.

5. Collaboration Tools: Cloud-based tools like Basecamp, Asana, and Microsoft SharePoint aid in file sharing, issue tracking, and workflow management.

6. Enterprise Project Management Software: Suitable for organizations managing multiple large projects simultaneously, offering resource management, risk tracking, and document libraries.

Consider factors like organizational culture, budget, project methodologies, project volume, and complexity when choosing software.

Initiate a project

Project initiation secures commitment to proceed. The process often begins with appointing a project manager. Sometimes, this step occurs after project approval, in which case the project manager must review and address any skipped or unfinished initiation activities. A critical part of initiation is defining the project, including problem identification, project objectives, requirements, and deliverables. Subsequently, a project charter is prepared to formally authorize the project and outline the project manager's authority.

Identify project stakeholders

As a project manager, it's crucial to identify and understand your project's stakeholders, which include the customer, project sponsor, involved departments, and project team members. Recognizing their roles and importance allows you to cultivate relationships with influential stakeholders, ensuring their satisfaction with project outcomes. Stakeholders can be categorized into major roles. The project customer, typically overseeing the problem to be solved, funds the project, defines its scope, and approves deliverables. A project sponsor, often an authoritative figure who supports project success, can assist in prioritizing objectives and addressing unsupportive stakeholders. Functional or aligned managers oversee departments and staff, impacting team composition. Project team members' jobs rely on their assignments and performance. Additionally, departments or individuals that influence or are affected by the project are considered stakeholders. Identifying and understanding stakeholders is essential for effective project management.

Analyze project stakeholders

Identifying and managing project stakeholders, understanding their significance, and determining effective ways to engage with them can be a complex task. A stakeholder analysis document serves as a valuable tool for storing information as you progressively identify and comprehend the roles of stakeholders in your project. This process evolves throughout the project definition phase. Begin by establishing the stakeholder's organizational affiliation and their position within it. Then, ascertain who influences the stakeholder, aiding in your approach when dealing with them. Identifying the project objectives that matter to the stakeholder and how they prioritize them provides insight into which stakeholders to engage if objective-related issues arise. Categorize stakeholders based on their influence and interest, aiding in prioritization. Lastly, document the stakeholder's contributions to the project, clarifying expectations or identifying go-to individuals. Utilize the provided stakeholder analysis spreadsheet to practice and input information about stakeholders in your projects. Effective stakeholder analysis during project initiation is essential for streamlining stakeholder management and ensuring their satisfaction with project outcomes.

Identify the project goal

The initial step in achieving project success is determining the customer's true requirements. The project goal represents the desired outcome, whether it's a problem to solve or an opportunity to seize, steering all project activities. Hence, precise definition is crucial. Begin by crafting a concise problem statement that outlines the core issue or opportunity. Avoid overcomplication; a single sentence is ideal. Constructing an accurate problem statement can be challenging, as people often rush into proposing solutions instead of identifying the initial problem or opportunity. In such cases, you can backtrack from a proposed solution to the root problem by repeatedly asking 'why.' This approach can unveil specific project objectives or refine the problem.

For instance, suppose a hospital's COO suggests implementing a new scheduling system. By probing deeper and asking 'why,' you might discover that existing scheduling inadequacies hinder resource utilization. Moreover, the hospital has acquired funding for enhancements. The resulting problem statement could be: Hospital resources are inefficiently utilized due to inadequate scheduling that fails to ensure availability of necessary equipment, staff, and facilities. Funding is accessible to address these scheduling issues. With a well-defined problem statement, you can establish the project goal, a clear and comprehensible target guiding team efforts and gaining buy-in, paving the path to project success. In the hospital project, the goal might be: The project aims to enhance scheduling to optimize hospital resource allocation, leveraging available funds for productivity and technological enhancements. Knowing your destination is the key to project commencement.

Define project objectives

Once the project goal is established, you can elaborate on it by pinpointing specific objectives. These objectives play a vital role in outlining the project's scope, chosen approach, and the criteria for success. Business objectives support your organization's overarching goals, such as achieving a 25% increase in market share or delivering top-tier healthcare. Financial objectives center around monetary aspects, such as boosting revenue by 15% or reducing costs by 10%. Quality objectives define the level of excellence required, like an 80% decrease in staph infections or a 75% reduction in readmissions for a hospital project. Technical objectives resemble specifications for equipment, like the need for mobile equipment usable in various medical settings. There's also a broader category known as performance, which might include time-related objectives like completing the project before the government grants expire on December 31st, 2030.

To effectively document objectives, it's advisable to adhere to SMART criteria. Specific objectives are crystal clear, leaving no room for ambiguity. For instance, "increase revenue by 15%." Measurable objectives facilitate clear assessment of their achievement; for instance, tracking reduced readmissions or revenue growth. Achievable and realistic objectives consider available resources, ensuring they are attainable without demoralizing the team. Lastly, time-related objectives set a definite target date, such as the government grants' deadline.

Once the project goal and objectives are identified, a benefit analysis with relevant stakeholders ensures alignment with the organization's mission and strategy while delivering anticipated business value. Multiple strategies exist to achieve project goals and objectives, with the selection typically initiated by senior project managers. However, it often begins with a brainstorming session involving a knowledgeable project team, followed by an evaluation of each strategy's alignment with project objectives. Project objectives play a crucial role in defining the project's scope, approach, and success criteria.

Gather requirements

Now that you've established the project goal, objectives, and strategy, the next step is to outline the specific deliverables, known as requirements. Accurate identification of requirements is crucial. Failure to identify a project's genuine requirements will lead to stakeholder dissatisfaction, while including unnecessary requirements can inflate project time and cost. For the hospital scheduling project, where one objective is to reduce procedure rescheduling by 75%, a requirement for the scheduling system could be simultaneous scheduling of staff, equipment, and facilities for a procedure. Another requirement could involve searching for the next available time slot accommodating all selected items. These requirements are not only essential but also precise, offering room for further elaboration.

Gathering requirements can pose challenges. Stakeholders may misinterpret or provide inconsistent, contradictory, or incomplete requirements. Sometimes non-stakeholders may attempt to insert their demands into your project. Moreover, stakeholders may hesitate to invest the necessary time for requirement definition.

Various techniques are available for gathering requirements. Interviews are effective when you approach the right people with well-prepared questions. Brainstorming sessions or focus groups comprising representatives from relevant groups can help gather department-specific requirements. Observing people's daily activities is another approach, allowing you to witness their work processes. Questionnaires and surveys are also useful, provided the questions are carefully crafted to avoid influencing responses. Analyzing existing documents or reverse engineering products can reveal requirements when documentation or results are available.

Following requirement gathering, it's essential to analyze the initial requirements to ensure coherence, consistency, and lack of duplication. Additional rounds of questioning and clarification may be necessary to refine the requirements. Once the requirements align and make sense, they should be documented in clear, easily understandable language. Organizing requirements into related categories can aid in eliminating duplication and conflicts. Requirements offer detailed descriptions of the project's deliverables, underscoring the importance of their accuracy.

For practice, consider the techniques you would employ to gather requirements for the hospital scheduling project and how you'd address potential challenges.

Identify project deliverables and success criteria

In essence, project deliverables are the outcomes a project produces, and to assess their appropriateness, you require measurable standards known as success criteria. Deliverables can take the form of tangible items such as a building, a new product, or a service, or they may be more abstract, such as enhanced performance, like a reduction in reported errors. These deliverables play a crucial role in defining the project scope, which specifies what is and isn't within the project's boundaries. Additionally, deliverables serve as yardsticks to gauge project progress during its execution.

To document project deliverables, start by enumerating the end deliverables, which are the final results your project delivers upon completion. For instance, an end deliverable for the scheduling project would be the "launch of a new scheduling system and processes." Next, record intermediate deliverables, which are accomplished throughout the project's duration. An intermediate deliverable for the scheduling project might involve signing a contract with the scheduling system vendor. It's important to note that intermediate deliverables don't necessarily require approval from the project customer. Aim to define deliverables that can be achieved between status reports, enabling progress assessment based on deliverables completed since the last report.

Now that you've identified your deliverables, it's essential to determine whether the ones you receive align with stakeholder expectations. To accomplish this, you need quantifiable criteria for measurement, known as success criteria. Success criteria serve as precise definitions of what constitutes success. While some criteria are straightforward, like signed vendor contracts or a building's certificate of occupancy, others may be subjective. To be effective, formulate clear and quantifiable success criteria. For instance, for the scheduling project, you could define success in terms of increased customer satisfaction as achieving a four out of five rating on customer surveys.

Deliverables represent the intended outcomes of your project, and success criteria enable you to ascertain their suitability. For practice, try identifying both end and intermediate deliverables for the hospital scheduling project, and then establish clear and quantifiable success criteria.

Identify project assumptions and risks

Another aspect of project definition involves pinpointing project assumptions and risks. Let's begin with assumptions. During project initiation, you may lack some essential information. However, you can make assumptions to move the project forward. As the project's details become clearer, you can revisit and adjust your assumptions as needed. For example, in the scheduling project, you might assume minimal system customization until you select a vendor, which could impact the required in-house resources and project duration. However, assumptions can be tricky when people unknowingly rely on them, assuming something is true without confirmation. This can lead to differing assumptions among team members, potentially causing disappointments or missed deadlines. To prevent this, bring assumptions into the open and ensure alignment among all stakeholders. When defining and planning the project, actively inquire about expectations and visions to uncover any unspoken assumptions.

Now, let's explore risks. Risks are uncertain situations or events that could impact your project, either positively or negatively. The defining characteristic of a risk is its uncertainty. Early in the project, dedicate time to identifying potential risks, primarily to enable the management team to make informed decisions about project investment. If numerous risks emerge, particularly concerning ones, management might opt for an alternative project. It's crucial to manage assumptions and risks by identifying them upfront. For practice, try identifying a few assumptions and risks that may arise in the hospital scheduling project.

Prepare a project scope statement

After defining your project, it's crucial to document the project scope. The project scope defines what's included in the project and, just as importantly, what's not included. Putting the project scope in writing is essential to prevent scope creep, which occurs when stakeholders request additional tasks without proper change management. Additionally, having the project scope in writing serves as a reference to remind stakeholders of their initial agreement. If someone questions what was agreed upon, you can refer back to the scope statement and clarify any items that are out of scope. A scope statement encompasses various aspects from project initiation, such as goals, objectives, deliverables, success criteria, assumptions, risks, and constraints.

For example, in the hospital scheduling project, the scope statement specifies what's within scope and what's out of scope. It clarifies that updating the staff assignment system and scheduling resident rooms are out of scope. Effectively managing scope is crucial for project success.

Create a project charter

With the project definition and scope statement completed, it's time to seek approval for project planning and create a project charter to formally authorize and announce the project. The purpose of defining the project is to provide the necessary information for project approval, which varies among organizations. Typically, the project undergoes a review against acceptance criteria aligned with the organization's goals. The review can result in three outcomes: approval to proceed with planning, denial, or the need for revisions.

When the project gains approval, the final step in initiation is to craft and distribute a project charter. This document serves to authorize and publicize the project. A typical project charter includes:

1. Project name.

2. Project purpose, along with a concise summary of its goals and objectives.

3. High-level project description, which may encompass success criteria, requirements, scope, risks, assumptions, and constraints.

4. Milestone schedule and cost estimate.

5. List of stakeholders.

6. Project manager's information, including name, responsibilities, extent of authority, and specific authorized actions (e.g., resource requests or contract signing).

7. A formal declaration of the sponsor's support for the project.

The project charter outlines the project manager's authority because their authority is project-specific and temporary, differing from the authority of structured organization managers. Thus, it is crucial that stakeholders understand the project manager's authorized actions. Once the project charter is ready, the project sponsor distributes it to all those affected by or involved in the project. With project authorization and recognition of the project manager's authority, project planning can commence.

Project planning overview

Project management involves detailed project planning, starting with the identification of necessary tasks. These tasks are broken down into manageable units. Once a task list is created, you can estimate workforce allocation, task durations, and associated costs. Creating a schedule involves considering task dependencies, resource availability, and timing.

Planning encompasses project execution methods, team communication strategies, tool selection, and frequency of communication. Additionally, you'll develop plans for change and risk management, as well as quality assurance. All these details are documented in the project plan.

The project plan isn't a static document; it's a dynamic tool used throughout the project's lifespan. It guides team members, tracks project progress, allows for development corrections, and facilitates stakeholder communication. The subsequent sections will delve into each element of a project plan, with a dedicated chapter focused on constructing a project schedule.

What is a work breakdown structure?

After receiving project approval, the initial step is to identify the project's required tasks. Even seemingly small projects can involve numerous tasks. Project managers utilize a Work Breakdown Structure (WBS) diagram to organize these tasks. The WBS divides the project work into manageable segments, facilitating planning, tracking, and management.

Creating a WBS offers several benefits:

1. Improved Estimations: Smaller work units make it easier to estimate time and costs. When estimating the entire project at once is challenging, breaking it into smaller parts allows for more accurate predictions.

2. Efficient Task Assignment: Smaller work units enable more efficient assignment of tasks to team members.

3. Progress Tracking: The WBS provides built-in checkpoints for measuring project progress.

A WBS comprises two types of tasks:

- Summary Tasks: These higher-level tasks provide an overview of project segments, which could represent phases, deliverables, or different organizational groups involved. The number of summary task levels depends on the project's complexity.

- Work Packages: These are the lowest-level tasks within the WBS, outlining detailed actions required to produce the lowest-level project deliverables.

By breaking down the project into manageable components, project planning and management become more effective and organized.

Build a work breakdown structure

To create an effective Work Breakdown Structure (WBS), start at the highest summary task level and work your way down. Collaborate with your team to identify the WBS, ensuring comprehensive coverage of project tasks and team buy-in. Begin by defining the top-level summary tasks as a team. Then delegate smaller groups to further decompose these summary tasks. Finally, conduct a collective review to address any issues.

If the full team is not yet onboard, initiate the WBS with your initial team, and later revise and add more detail as additional members join. Utilize the scope statement and deliverables to identify top-level summary tasks. For instance, if the project's scope includes redesigning scheduling processes, implementing a new scheduling system, creating documentation, and providing training, create summary tasks for each of these components.

Break down these summary tasks into smaller components, guided by intermediate deliverables as needed. For instance, if the project includes a deliverable for a signed contract with a system vendor, tasks like obtaining proposals, selecting the vendor, negotiating terms, and signing the contract can be added.

To determine the appropriate level of decomposition, aim for work packages that require between eight and 80 hours to complete, matching the frequency of status reports. Ensure that task durations are shorter than reporting periods and that the level of detail is manageable. Different project segments may warrant varying levels of decomposition, so adjust as needed.

Don't fret over the initial WBS organization; it can be rearranged as you gain more insights into the project. Starting from the top down is effective, using the scope statement and deliverables as initial guides. For practice, try expanding the scheduling project's WBS based on its scope and deliverables.

How to create work packages

Creating a brief task name in a Work Breakdown Structure (WBS) is insufficient for guiding team members on their responsibilities. To provide your team with the necessary information, develop work package documents that offer detailed descriptions of the tasks. The level of detail required in these documents varies based on factors such as the task's complexity and the team member's experience.

For instance, less experienced individuals may need comprehensive descriptions, while more experienced team members might only require task checklists. If detailed task information exists in another document, you can reference that source.

A work package document serves not only to describe the task but also to specify how its completion and correctness will be assessed. In some cases, you can incorporate the related deliverable and success criteria within the work package document. If not, create a description of the expected outcome upon task completion.

Since you may not possess sufficient expertise in every aspect of the work as a project manager, enlist the help of those who contributed to the WBS, team leaders of involved groups, or other knowledgeable individuals to fill in the details. Work packages are instrumental in assisting team members in fulfilling their responsibilities.

Estimate time and cost

The two most common questions about a project are usually, "How long will it take?" and "How much will it cost?" Precise estimation is crucial because it can influence whether the project is viable. Initially, you estimate the time required as it impacts both the project's schedule and cost. You also estimate non-time-based costs like materials and additional expenses such as travel.

During the project's initiation and planning phases, you may collaborate with a core planning team to establish initial estimates. As the project progresses into execution, more accurate estimates can be obtained from team members responsible for specific tasks. They possess the necessary expertise and motivation to provide reliable estimates. Initial estimates don't need to be perfect; for project selection, an estimate with an accuracy range of plus or minus 75% might suffice. As the project is further defined during planning, the aim is to improve accuracy to plus or minus 10%.

Various estimation techniques are available. For projects resembling ones previously completed, using them as a reference can be helpful. Parametric models involve calculating work and costs based on measurable factors like square footage for construction, especially when data from similar projects exist. In situations where the project is unfamiliar territory for the organization, consider consulting experts, such as consultants or vendors who are well-versed in the field.

The Delphi Technique relies on multiple experts offering independent estimates, with their identities kept anonymous to avoid undue influence. Averaging the estimates from the final round yields the final estimated value. For larger projects or rough estimates, top-down estimation is effective, beginning with estimates for phases or major components and then breaking them down into smaller tasks. Bottom-up estimation involves estimating each task individually and aggregating them for the overall project estimate. You can also combine these approaches as needed.

Given what you know about the hospital scheduling project, consider which estimation technique you would choose and the level of accuracy you would aim for in your estimate.

How to choose the best estimate

Project estimates can be likened to your daily commute; you aim for an estimate that ensures you reach your destination on time. Typically, your commute may take around 45 minutes, with occasional variations due to unforeseen incidents. To play it safe, you select a time that allows for flexibility.

Similarly, project estimates require a systematic approach. Consider a bell curve, representing a normal distribution, where your average estimate is at the peak. Here, 50% of values are below the average, and 50% are above it. Thus, providing the average estimate gives you a 50-50 chance of success or failure, which might not be the best bet.

Conversely, the worst-case estimate maximizes the chance of success but may cause the project to be canceled due to excessive caution. Customers often ask about best-case scenarios, but falling into that trap can set up unrealistic expectations.

The sweet spot lies approximately halfway between the average and worst-case values on the bell curve, granting an 86% probability of success. You can adjust this value higher for added safety or lower for increased risk, depending on the project's circumstances. In essence, choose an estimate that aligns with an acceptable probability of success.

Create a resource management plan

Planning involves defining project roles, responsibilities, and resource management. This includes creating a resource management plan, which encompasses a staffing plan and responsibility matrix.

The responsibility matrix outlines decision-making authority and communication within the project. It classifies responsibilities into four categories: R (Responsible), I (Inform), C (Consult), and A (Accountable). During planning, review and resolve any discrepancies with stakeholders and identify areas without clear ownership.

The project organization chart establishes the hierarchy and reporting structure for project participants, aiding in communication and escalation of issues.

Identify necessary skills and quantities using a skills matrix. Match required skills with project tasks, estimate the number of resources needed, and calculate labor costs.

Lastly, develop a detailed staffing plan that specifies resource sources (in-house, outsourced, contracted), resource timing, required training, and resource-related processes for onboarding, task assignment, progress tracking, and project release. The resource management plan comprehensively documents roles, responsibilities, resource needs, and management procedures.

Build a project schedule

A Work Breakdown Structure (WBS) identifies project tasks but doesn't provide timing or sequencing information. To create a schedule:

1. Organize tasks in the right order, considering task dependencies where one must finish before another starts (e.g., "Build Specs" before "Review Specs").

2. Estimate the time required for each task, which, along with task sequence, determines the project's duration.

3. Assign team members to tasks to calculate task durations.

4. Account for constraints like deadlines and resource availability.

Adjust the schedule as needed to meet project goals. The schedule is a crucial project aspect, determining project duration and resource needs.

Develop a project budget

Money is a critical aspect of most projects, and managing project costs is vital. The project budget serves as your initial reference point. It must realistically estimate the project's total cost, including labor, materials, and various expenses like travel.

Labor costs, covering employees and vendors, constitute a significant portion of project expenses. Employee costs should include salaries and benefits. Other time-based resources, such as rented equipment or office space, also factor into the calculations.

Material costs, like servers or training materials, must be accounted for. Additionally, consider other miscellaneous costs such as travel, training, and fees.

To avoid cash flow issues, determine when project expenses will arise. This helps ensure you stay within your allocated budget, making adjustments as needed to reduce costs, potentially by eliminating non-essential items, seeking additional funding, or finding cost-effective alternatives. The project budget serves as your cost target throughout the project.

Consider solutions for the $100,000 exceeding the allocated budget for the scheduling project.

Identify risks

After thorough project planning, the next crucial step is risk planning because unforeseen issues are bound to arise. Rather than seeking excitement, it's wiser to proactively identify potential problems and develop strategies to address them.

Let's start with the known risks, referred to as "known unknowns." These are risks you are aware of, such as weather delays or resource unavailability. For instance, factors like technology can pose risks due to unexpected costs, malfunctions, or delays. Geographically dispersed project teams may introduce risks related to time zones, language barriers, or a lack of team cohesion. Insufficient project details, such as vague deliverables, deadlines, or team assignments, can lead to various issues. Limited options, such as individuals with rare skills, increase risk because suitable alternatives may be hard to find.

To identify risks, collaborate with your team, consult experts in relevant project areas, gather insights from key project stakeholders, and seek input from other experienced project managers. Document each risk thoroughly using a risk information form, including information on affected objectives, triggering events, consequences, responsible parties, and more.

Now, what about unforeseeable risks, known as "unknown unknowns"? These stem from highly unlikely situations that may not even cross your mind. While you may not encounter major unknown risks like natural disasters, smaller unknown risks are inevitable. To prepare for them, allocate contingency funds and time. The exact amount can vary but is often determined as a percentage of the project budget, typically around 15%, based on historical data.

To minimize the impact of risks, the first step is to identify potential risks your hospital scheduling project might face.

Create a risk management plan

A risk management plan outlines which risks to focus on and how to address them effectively. Start by assessing risks based on their likelihood and potential impact, using a scale of one to five, where one signifies low likelihood or impact, and five represents high likelihood or severe impact. Calculate a risk score by multiplying the probability and impact, and focus on managing risks with a score of nine or higher.

Plan your risk responses according to the following strategies:

1. Acceptance: Accept the consequences for low-probability, low-impact risks.

2. Avoidance: Modify the project scope to eliminate or minimize risky components.

3. Mitigation: Take actions to reduce the consequences or impact of the risk, such as feasibility studies.

4. Transfer: Shift the risk to another party, like purchasing insurance, which reduces but doesn't eliminate risk.

Ensure your responses are proportionate to the risks, considering factors like cost-effectiveness. Remember that contingency time and funds can address unforeseen risks or those initially overlooked.

Lastly, establish a system for monitoring risks and evaluating responses. Maintain a risk log detailing risk description, triggers, probability, impact, chosen responses, responsible parties, expected outcomes, and risk status. Regularly update the risk plan to adapt to changing project circumstances and track the effectiveness of responses. A risk management plan safeguards your project from potential issues.

Set up a communication plan

Effective communication is vital for project success. Establishing a communication plan ensures that the right information reaches the right people at the right time and in the right manner. Begin by identifying your project's key audiences, referring to the responsibility matrix for guidance.

1. Audiences: Determine who needs project information, such as management stakeholders, the project sponsor, functional managers, and team members.

2. Information Needs: Understand what each audience requires. Management stakeholders may seek project objectives, while functional managers need details on skill sets and timelines.

3. Communication Methods: Choose suitable communication methods and frequencies. Face-to-face meetings are ideal for brainstorming and sensitive topics, while email, conference calls, and video conferencing are essential for geographically dispersed teams.

By crafting a communication plan, you ensure stakeholders receive essential information effectively, contributing to stakeholder management and overall project success. Apply this approach to the Hospital Scheduling Project for better project communication.

Develop a quality plan

Project success means achieving objectives without exceeding them. Quality management ensures that a project meets its objectives and requirements. A quality management plan serves as a guide to reach these goals. Project quality is about meeting customer requirements, adhering to schedules, and staying within budget. For deliverables and products, quality involves adhering to specifications.

A quality management plan comprises three parts:

1. Quality Standards for Deliverables: These standards define acceptable criteria for products or deliverables. For example, the scheduling system must meet all required scheduling functions.

2. Quality Assurance Plan: This outlines processes used throughout the project to ensure final results meet quality standards. It may include requirements and design reviews and software testing during development.

3. Quality Control: This part explains how you'll measure and monitor quality in the final deliverables, ensuring they meet the established standards. This involves examining or measuring results against set standards.

Continuous improvement is integral to quality management. Tools like cause-and-effect diagrams and Pareto diagrams help identify factors contributing to problems and prioritize solutions. By developing a quality management plan, you can ensure that your project consistently achieves its quality objectives.

How to set up a change management plan

The tax code, once simple, has become complex due to numerous changes. Managing changes is essential, and a Change Management Plan helps incorporate vital changes into your project while excluding unnecessary ones. Here's how it works:

1. Identify What to Control: Determine what aspects of the project you want to manage, such as project scope, requirements, schedule, or the entire project plan. These controlled versions are known as baseline documents.

2. Establish a Change Review Board: This group consists of key stakeholders who review change requests and decide whether to approve them.

3. Define a Change Management Process: The specific process you choose depends on factors like company culture and project size. The typical components include:

  - Documenting and Submitting a Change Request: Use a standardized form to gather necessary information about the requested change, including its reason, business justification, and expected results.

  - Evaluation of the Change: An assigned team member assesses the change's necessity, proposed approach, effort, cost, impact, and potential risks.

  - Change Review Board's Review: The board accepts, rejects, or requests revisions to change requests. They communicate decisions to requesters.

  - Updating Baseline Documents: Approved changes are incorporated into baseline documents, such as project schedules.

  - Tracking Change Requests: Maintain a log to monitor change request statuses, responsible individuals, impact estimates, and actual outcomes.

Set thresholds for handling smaller change requests and establish a process for emergency changes that require rapid decisions between Change Review Board meetings. A Change Management Plan ensures that your project incorporates meaningful changes while preventing it from being overwhelmed by unnecessary ones.

How to plan procurement

Just as you don't start from scratch when making homemade chicken soup, in projects, it's often more efficient to procure items, services, and skills externally. This necessitates a procurement plan:

1. Identify Needs: Determine what you need to procure, such as specific skills, additional personnel, or materials.

2. Document Procurement Processes: Specify who handles procurement (e.g., purchasing department or project team), outline vendor selection criteria, describe the selection process, contract types, and contract management

methods. Leverage existing organizational procurement processes where possible.

3. Make-or-Buy Decision Process: Explain how you decide whether to produce in-house or procure externally. Start by clarifying requirements, prioritizing them, and evaluating available products or services against these needs. Consider the advantages and disadvantages of making versus buying. Tight timelines often favor procurement.

4. Vendor List: Compile a list of potential vendors, outlining how you researched and selected them based on specific criteria.

Procurement planning helps you make informed decisions about what to procure, and if necessary, which products and services to procure. For practice, outline the criteria for selecting a scheduling system vendor.

How to obtain approval to proceed

To gain stakeholder approval for your project plan, a face-to-face sign-off meeting is more effective than simply mailing or emailing the plan for signatures. This approach ensures stakeholders understand and agree with the plan. Here's how it works:

1. Schedule a sign-off meeting with stakeholders to present the project plan.

2. Address any issues or concerns immediately during the meeting.

3. Once everyone agrees, have stakeholders sign a signature page to indicate their approval.

If in-person meetings are not possible, video conferences or conference calls can be used, and remote participants can transmit their signatures via fax, email, or mail. The goal is to ensure stakeholder understanding and commitment to the project, rather than relying solely on signatures as legal documents.

Put tasks in sequence

Creating a schedule involves arranging tasks in the right order, similar to cooking dinner before eating it. This sequencing of tasks is visualized using a network diagram in project management. Each task is represented in a box with relevant information, and arrows connecting the boxes indicate task sequences.

Task dependencies are crucial in establishing the order of tasks. There are four types of task dependencies:

1. Finish-to-Start (FS): The finish of one task dictates the start of another. For example, analyzing current scheduling processes must finish before designing new ones can start.

2. Finish-to-Finish (FF): The finish of one task controls the finish of another, possibly with a slight delay. For instance, development completion triggers testing, allowing a small delay for customization testing.

3. Start-to-Start (SS): The start of one task initiates the start of another. However, this can lead to issues if the predecessor takes longer than expected.

4. Start-to-Finish (SF): This dependency type is rare and can be confusing. The start of one task determines the finish of another, causing the controlled task to finish after its controller.

To determine the appropriate dependency type, consider which task controls the other (predecessor), whether it's the start or finish date of the first task that controls the second task, and whether the predecessor controls the start or finish of the successor. Incorporating task dependencies into your network diagram ensures task sequencing in your project.

How to assign resources to tasks

Once your project tasks are sequenced and their durations estimated, the final scheduling element involves resource allocation. This step determines task durations and their timing based on resource availability. Resources are typically assigned to work packages, representing essential tasks in your work breakdown structure (WBS). Summary tasks and milestones don't receive resource assignments.

The impact of assigning resources to work packages depends on whether you estimate task duration or work. When estimating duration and allocating resources, your scheduling tool calculates the work output based on the allocated resources and task duration. For instance, if you estimate a two-week duration for a task and assign two full-time vendor resources, it equals 160 hours of work.

On the other hand, if you estimate work, your scheduling tool uses the work estimate and resource allocation to calculate the task duration. Some tasks, like meetings, maintain their duration regardless of the number of assigned resources. For instance, a four-hour meeting remains four hours long, whether attended by three or ten people.

Resource availability also impacts task timing. If your schedule indicates equipment installation starting on December 9th, but IT resources won't be available until December 18th due to prior commitments, you'll need to delay the task accordingly.

Remember to allocate various resource types, including materials, equipment, and additional costs. With all resources assigned, you'll gain a clearer understanding of your project's schedule.

Learn to use milestones

Milestones in projects serve as markers of key progress points, unlike the historical road markers they're named after. They indicate the completion of significant tasks or project segments, offering a visual gauge of how much is accomplished and when.

Milestones are most effective as the initial and final tasks in your project schedule. Starting with a milestone allows you to adjust the project's start date simply by moving this starting marker to a later date. The final milestone indicates whether the project is on schedule, delayed, or ahead.

These markers also highlight interim progress during a project, serving as satisfying checkpoints when all preceding work is completed. If you're dependent on external deliveries, consider adding a milestone to signal their importance. Additionally, milestones can represent critical decisions or approvals that dictate the project's next steps.

Incorporating milestones into your project schedule helps track progress and provides flexibility for rescheduling specific project components when necessary.

Make a realistic schedule

Ensuring your project schedule is realistic is crucial to align tasks closely with your planned dates. Here's how to inject realism into your schedule:

1. Estimate task duration based on actual work hours people can dedicate to the project each day. Recognize that not all work hours are fully productive due to meetings, paperwork, training, and other distractions.

2. Adjust estimated task hours to account for the efficiency and speed of assigned workers. If someone is exceptionally skilled in a particular area, modify the task work hours to reflect their productivity.

3. Maintain productivity by limiting each resource to work on no more than three tasks concurrently. Frequent task-switching introduces small delays, so adjust resource assignments accordingly when dealing with high-demand situations.

Always document any adjustments made to your schedule, along with the reasons behind them. This documentation will prove invaluable when addressing future changes or challenges. The more closely your resource assignments mirror reality, the better your chances of keeping the project on track.

Understand the critical path

The critical path in your project schedule is crucial because it represents the longest sequence of tasks. Any delay in these critical tasks directly impacts the project's finish date. Conversely, shortening the critical path results in a shorter project schedule. Identifying critical tasks is straightforward; they have no slack or float, meaning they can't be delayed without pushing back the project's finish date.

To determine if a task has slack, you examine its early start, early finish, late start, and late finish dates. Early start and early finish are the earliest possible task start and finish dates based on dependencies, calculated using a forward pass. Conversely, late start and late finish represent the latest possible dates without delaying subsequent tasks and are determined through a backward pass calculation.

Critical tasks have no slack, meaning their early and late dates are identical. Project scheduling software can efficiently calculate the critical path for you. Monitoring and managing tasks on the critical path are key to keeping your project on schedule or even delivering it ahead of time.

How to shorten a schedule

Stakeholders often seek quicker project delivery, and there are strategies for shortening project schedules. One approach is fast tracking, which involves overlapping tasks that typically follow a sequential order. For instance, you can begin designing software features before completing the system design to expedite the project. Fast tracking simplifies by adding an overlap to tasks with finish-to-start dependencies. To achieve the most significant schedule reduction, focus on fast tracking the longest tasks along the critical path, as it minimizes risks and changes.

However, fast tracking comes with increased risks, such as potential rework due to design changes. Another technique, crashing, requires investing additional resources or funds to speed up the schedule. Tasks along the critical path are the primary targets for crashing, as it makes no sense to spend resources on tasks that won't impact the schedule. Begin with the least expensive tasks and progress to more costly ones. Select tasks based on the lowest crash cost per week, and if multiple tasks have the same cost, prioritize the longer ones.

It's crucial to remember that crashing has its limits, as too many resources can lead to inefficiencies and reduced productivity. Always reassess the critical path after making adjustments to ensure it remains accurate.

The third method for schedule reduction is cutting project scope. Removing tasks on the critical path shortens the schedule. Each technique, whether fast tracking, crashing, or scope reduction, comes with its advantages and disadvantages. The choice of which method to employ should align with the specific project's needs and constraints. Consider which techniques would be suitable for the scheduling project and identify the relevant tasks involved.

Document the baseline

After stakeholders approve the project plan, it's time to establish the project baseline, which comprises approved project documents such as requirements, schedules, budgets, and spreadsheets. These baseline documents serve as the foundation for control through the Change Management Process. By comparing actual project performance to the baseline, you can assess how the project is progressing. Any changes to baseline documents trigger change requests because the baseline is subject to control.

Defining the baseline depends on what you're specifying. Initially, save the baseline version of plan documents, and if changes occur, highlight those modifications in a revised baseline document. For project schedules, most scheduling programs offer a feature to save a baseline, which includes approved values for start and finish dates, task duration, work, cost, and more. As you record progress or make adjustments to the schedule, the program will indicate any deviations from the baseline.

Once you have documented the project baseline, you can utilize it to evaluate progress and project performance. To practice, determine which documents should be included in the scheduling project baseline and consider where to store them for convenient access.

What is agile project management?

Agile projects are ideal for situations where business requirements evolve frequently or when the business seeks rapid value delivery. Agile achieves this by regularly delivering small product components known as features. This continuous release of deliverables necessitates a distinct approach to project management and execution, known as Agile Project Management.

In Agile, work is organized into time-bound iterations or sprints, typically lasting two to 12 weeks. Each iteration aims to deliver a fully functional feature, enabling quicker value realization. Agile emphasizes human interactions and collaboration over strict processes and tools. Communication occurs as needed, fostering collaboration between business and technical team members, who may work in the same location or utilize collaborative tools.

Agile prioritizes product development over excessive documentation, with documentation tailored to the team's immediate requirements. Customer engagement is heightened in Agile projects, with continuous collaboration throughout the development process, making it easier to meet evolving needs. Changes are not only expected but encouraged, as Agile views change as an opportunity to enhance value.

Agile encompasses many of the same activities as traditional waterfall project management but in a different sequence. While the waterfall approach defines scope first and then estimates time, cost, and quality, Agile considers time, cost, and quality as fixed parameters. Agile focuses on determining which features can be delivered within these constraints.

The Agile methodology follows stages like envision, speculate, explore, adapt, and close to develop and test features. Change control involves prioritizing feature backlogs, and risk management is achieved through frequent releases. Agile is not limited to IT projects; it can be applied to non-IT projects as long as deliverables can be produced and implemented in short cycles.

For practice, identify parts of the hospital scheduling project that could benefit from an Agile approach.

The agile project management lifecycle

Agile development involves key activities such as sprint planning, daily scrum, sprint review, and sprint retrospective. However, when managing Agile work within a larger hybrid project, you can apply Agile project management principles as defined by Jim Highsmith.

Jim Highsmith's Agile project management life cycle consists of five stages: envision, speculate, explore, adapt, and close. These stages seamlessly integrate into the project management framework and Agile development approach.

The envision stage marks the project's outset, where you collaborate with the customer to define project goals, objectives, and team composition. This stage also establishes project guidelines, such as problem-solving approaches, collaboration methods, and working hours. It results in a comprehensive project definition, including customer goals, objectives, scope, and stakeholders.

In contrast to the waterfall approach, Agile projects continually cycle through the speculate, explore, and adapt stages for each iteration. The speculate stage involves planning at the iteration level, focusing on identifying business functions, developing features, estimating effort, and addressing associated risks. This leads to the explore stage, where the team constructs the iteration's features with frequent peer reviews and thorough testing. The adapt stage allows for feedback incorporation and issue resolution, with product owner or customer reviews and team meetings for reflection and lessons learned.

This iterative process continues until all features are complete or the allocated time and budget are exhausted. Upon feature completion, the close stage ensures that all tasks are finalized and captures additional lessons learned for future projects.

The Agile life cycle's repeated stages enable a faster start to feature development. Consider creating a schedule illustrating the Agile life cycle with four iterations for the hospital scheduling system project.

Plan an iteration

In Agile projects, planning is essential before diving into the work. During the speculate stage, both business and technical teams identify features for the current iteration. Features represent small functions or deliverables that address specific business needs. In the context of the hospital project, features could include scheduling functions, user documentation, and training materials. Features are typically named using an action-result convention, such as "find next available appointment time" or "change procedure room."

The initial speculate stage for the first iteration takes longer because it involves identifying and estimating all project features, collectively referred to as the backlog. One approach to building the backlog is to list each feature on sticky notes or index cards. Alternatively, Agile collaboration tools can be used to manage features. Once the feature list is complete, both business and technical teams review and prioritize them. Business teams prioritize based on functionality, while technical teams consider the optimal order for building features. The Agile approach accommodates changes and questions regarding features, with the possibility of deferring some to future projects if the list becomes extensive.

Additionally, during this stage, estimates are developed for all features in the project. After the prioritized feature list is approved by the customer or sponsor, you can create an iteration, milestone, and release plan. This plan outlines when features are scheduled for iterations and when they will be implemented in the organization. This marks the beginning of the explore stage for the first iteration.

As time progresses, an Agile project may deviate from the initial plan. During subsequent speculate stages, features need to be re-estimated, re-evaluated, and reprioritized. This includes reconsidering features that were not completed and have returned to the backlog, new features that have emerged since the initial backlog creation, and selecting the next features from the backlog for inclusion in the iteration. Despite these adjustments, the speculate stage is relatively short, often lasting a few days, especially for iterations of around three weeks. Each iteration begins with planning for the upcoming work.

Manage the explore stage

In Agile projects, the explore stage swiftly leads to feature building and implementation. During this stage, substantial collaboration takes place between the business and technical teams. The primary focus of the explore stage is working on the features assigned to the current iteration. Daily standup meetings, typically lasting 15 minutes, are crucial during this stage, where team members provide updates on their previous day's progress, what they plan to complete that day, and any assistance required. It's important to note that any issues raised during these meetings are not resolved on the spot; instead, they are noted for subsequent resolution, with updates provided in the next day's meeting. The only tangible output from these meetings is the addition of issues to a register for tracking lessons learned.

While the team manages these meetings, the project manager plays a role in removing obstacles hindering team members' work. During the meetings, the project manager tracks progress on the features scheduled for the current iteration and investigates any delays or issues, documenting them in an issue log. If any issues remain unresolved, the project manager offers assistance. If the meeting starts to deviate from its purpose, the project manager can step in to refocus the team's attention.

After the meetings, stakeholders are informed about the project's progress. A fundamental concept in the Agile approach is that work on features stops when the iteration's scheduled duration ends, regardless of whether the features are complete. Incomplete work is placed in the backlog for future iterations. Conversely, if the team completes the iteration's features faster than estimated, they can begin work on additional features from the backlog to utilize the remaining time.

In essence, the explore stage primarily involves feature development and implementation, complemented by brief daily meetings to maintain project alignment and progress tracking. For practical purposes, project managers can create checklists to ensure they monitor key aspects during daily standup meetings.

Handle the adapt and close stages

In the final stage of an iteration, the adapt stage serves as a time for review and reflection, akin to evaluating the past year and setting resolutions for improvement on New Year's Day. During this phase, you and the team compare the actual deliverables to the planned ones, discussing both successes and shortcomings. The team may identify adjustments to enhance the efficiency of future iterations.

Reviewing the work with the customer ensures that the features meet their intended functionality and deliver the anticipated business benefits. Additionally, a lessons learned session is essential for sharing feedback and brainstorming solutions for issues while capitalizing on successful aspects. This feedback can lead to changes in the next iteration's speculate stage, such as adding or removing features, modifying estimates, updating the risk register, or reprioritizing the backlog.

Furthermore, the adapt stage provides an opportunity to refine processes that may not be functioning optimally. Celebrating successes is encouraged at this juncture, and team members can briefly recharge to approach the next iteration with enthusiasm. If the project entails multiple iterations, the end of the adapt stage initiates the speculate stage for the subsequent iteration. However, if the project's schedule or budget has been exhausted, it's time for the close phase to tie up loose ends.

The close phase involves reconciling project financials, ensuring all invoices are settled, and closing project accounts to prevent inadvertent charges. Team member reassignment in coordination with resource managers is also essential. As in any project, communicating the project results to the customer and stakeholders is crucial. Concluding each iteration and the project overall ensures that the achievements are recognized, affirming the success of both the present and future projects.

For practical purposes, create agendas for the review meetings scheduled during the adapt stage of each iteration.

Kicking off and managing project work

After completing the planning phase and commencing the project, it's time to put your planning efforts into action as you work towards project completion. Execution involves assembling the necessary personnel and resources for project tasks. Once team members are onboard, they require clear assignments, team collaborations, and an understanding of the project's workflow, which is typically discussed in a kickoff meeting. During this meeting, the project sponsor and customer can outline the project's purpose, fostering enthusiasm among the team. Additionally, you can review the project plan, elucidating communication methods and change request procedures. A digital project notebook is set up to store project-related information, including plans, specifications, documents, and reports, ensuring accessibility for team members.

Subsequently, project execution encompasses the actual implementation of the tasks outlined in the work breakdown structure. The monitoring and controlling processes run concurrently with execution. Monitoring entails gathering data to assess the project's status, considering that projects often deviate from meticulously crafted plans. As changes, surprises, and challenges emerge, the project team must formulate responses. Controlling comes into play when adjustments are needed to steer the project back on its intended development.

Techniques for communicating effectively

As a project manager, effective communication is crucial as you interact with individuals at various organizational levels, from customers and management to project team members. Effective communication involves conveying messages in a way that ensures understanding and prompts action. Possessing strong communication skills is essential, as they enable you and your team to achieve higher-quality work more efficiently.

Here are key communication principles to follow:

1. Provide context: Begin by explaining why the message is important, grabbing the audience's attention.

2. Be concise: Get to the main point quickly to maintain the audience's interest.

3. Tailor the message: Customize your communication to the audience's interests and use terminology they understand.

4. Stay positive and proactive: When addressing issues, present a problem-solving plan alongside the problem itself.

Additional communication tips include active listening, avoiding distractions during conversations, being aware of non-verbal cues, favoring face-to-face discussions for critical matters, keeping an open mind, paraphrasing to ensure understanding, and using email effectively by crafting clear, well-structured messages. Proofreading emails is essential to avoid misunderstandings, and it's important to follow up if you don't receive a response. Lastly, proceed with caution when using humor in email, reserving it for situations where it's appropriate and well-received. For practice, create communication guidelines to share with your project team.

Run effective meetings

Meetings, although consuming time and resources, can sometimes be essential for effective communication and work. To ensure meetings are productive, follow these steps:

1. Define the purpose: Clearly identify the meeting's objectives and desired outcomes, such as gaining approval or resolving an issue.

2. Create an agenda: Outline discussion topics and include time estimates for each item. This keeps discussions focused and helps manage meeting time effectively.

3. Limit attendees: Invite only those necessary to achieve the meeting's goals, and allow attendees time to prepare by sending invitations and materials in advance.

4. Punctuality: Start and end meetings on time, even if not all attendees are present, to discourage tardiness.

5. Facilitate: Consider having someone else act as the facilitator to ensure the meeting stays on track, guiding discussions and enforcing ground rules.

6. Take comprehensive notes: Document decisions, action items, and responsible parties during the meeting. Afterward, edit the notes to emphasize action items and distribute them to attendees and relevant parties.

By running effective meetings, you can improve project management and enhance your reputation at work. To prepare, create a checklist of tasks to complete before holding a meeting.

Manage team resources

Motivating your project team members and strengthening your working relationships with them is essential for achieving project objectives. Here are key methods to achieve this:

1. Clarify Roles and Responsibilities: Clearly communicate each team member's role and responsibilities, helping them understand what is expected of them.

2. Set Specific Goals: Provide team members with clear, achievable goals that challenge them to excel.

3. Offer Support: Remove obstacles hindering their progress and provide support whenever necessary.

4. Show Respect: Demonstrate respect for your team members as valuable contributors to the project's success.

5. Provide Timely Feedback: Offer prompt, constructive feedback, both positive reinforcement and constructive guidance.

6. Honesty: Consistently tell the truth, fostering trust even when delivering difficult messages.

7. Regular Communication: Maintain open, regular communication with your team through status meetings and lessons learned sessions.

8. Address Issues Promptly: Handle any people-related problems swiftly and tactfully, offering guidance or seeking replacements when necessary.

By implementing these techniques, you can build effective working relationships and keep your team motivated. To reinforce your understanding, prepare a sample speech for your project kickoff meeting to communicate these principles to your team.

Understand team dynamics

When individuals come together to work on a project, they often go through several stages of team development. A well-known model for describing these phases is Bruce Tuckman's "Forming, Storming, Norming, and Performing." Here's a concise breakdown of each stage:

1. Forming: At the forming stage, individuals are just starting to come together as a team. They may be unsure about their team's goals and roles. As a leader, your role is to define the team's objectives and provide direction. Expect some resistance and questions as the team forms.

2. Storming: During the storming stage, team members start working out their relationships, which can lead to power struggles and disagreements. This phase can be challenging, but it also promotes communication and growth. Your role is to help the team stay focused on their goals and facilitate decision-making.

3. Norming: In the norming stage, the team begins to understand their common goal, and cooperation and collaboration become more natural. Team members work together to achieve success. This is a positive phase where the team is becoming more cohesive.

4. Performing: Not all teams reach the performing stage, but when they do, they work exceptionally well together. They understand their objectives, roles, and responsibilities, and they can achieve tasks efficiently without constant guidance.

Helping your team progress through these stages of development can enhance your project's efficiency and result in high-quality outcomes.

How to manage virtual teams

Managing virtual teams presents unique challenges due to geographical distances and limited face-to-face communication. Effective communication is essential to overcome these obstacles. Key strategies include:

1. Clear Communication: Ensure that your messages are clear and concise, minimizing room for misinterpretation, as you lack visual cues in virtual interactions.

2. Confirmation of Understanding: Encourage team members to confirm their understanding of instructions and information to avoid misunderstandings.

3. Support and Respect: Apply the same interpersonal skills you use in the office to build relationships with remote team members. Be supportive and respectful of their needs.

4. Obstacle Removal: Assist team members in overcoming obstacles that may hinder their productivity or communication.

5. Acknowledgment: Express gratitude and provide positive feedback to remote team members to motivate and recognize their efforts.

Conflict resolution can be more challenging in virtual teams, so opt for phone or video conferencing for sensitive discussions. Additionally, coordinate suitable meeting times to accommodate different time zones and establish clear communication protocols within the team.

Managing virtual teams requires adapting to these challenges while fostering effective communication and collaboration among remote team members.

How to gather data

While your project is in progress, it's crucial to monitor various aspects such as task start dates, actual work hours, remaining work, and costs. This includes tracking schedule and budget information, which are vital project metrics.

To effectively track progress, start by ensuring tasks commence as planned to avoid potential project delays. Collecting actual work hours, though it requires some effort, provides a more accurate insight into progress and labor costs. It's also essential to determine the remaining work or duration to assess if your initial estimates were accurate.

In addition to labor costs, remember to gather data on other expenses like travel, fees, and training. Consider automating data collection through methods like email, online forms, or enterprise reporting tools to streamline the process and free up your time for critical project management tasks.

Monitoring progress data helps you stay informed about your project's status and allows you to take necessary actions to keep it on task. For practice, design a data collection form tailored to the hospital scheduling project.

How to manage project change

During project planning, you created a change management plan to outline how project changes will be handled. Now that the project is in progress, it's time to implement that plan. When a change request is submitted, follow these steps:

1. Assign someone to assess the request, add it to the change request log, and submit it to the change review board.

2. Include your recommendation for approval or rejection in the submission.

3. If the request is rejected, promptly inform the requester and ensure no team members begin working on it without approval.

However, if the change request is approved:

4. Assign someone to monitor it and update baseline documents to reflect the change, such as tasks, project finish date, or cost increases.

5. Clearly tag baseline document edits with the change request number to track modifications.

6. The change request owner maintains the request's status in the change request log, reports on its progress, and oversees it until completion.

7. Finally, update the change request log with actual hours, costs, and any changes to the project finish date, if applicable.

In cases where a change request has a significant impact, exceptions to the standard approval process include:

- If the change request affects the project's business case, it requires approval from the customer.

- If a change request impacts other projects, it should be presented to the organization's executive board for approval.

For emergencies that can't wait for the regular change review board meeting, consider arranging an emergency review board meeting or seeking approval from the customer or sponsor. Managing change requests is crucial for keeping the project on track while approving those that align with project goals.

Learn how to manage project scope

Stakeholders may want to expand your project's scope as they learn more about it, but they may not be willing to adjust the budget or timeline accordingly. This phenomenon is known as scope creep, and it's essential to manage it.

Scope creep can occur when someone requests additional project elements without considering schedule or budget adjustments. To prevent scope creep, clearly define the scope during the planning phase. However, if scope creep starts to happen:

1. Address unrealistic expectations by pointing out that requested features are beyond the project's scope.

2. Discuss necessary schedule and budget changes with the customer when adding new elements.

3. Emphasize the importance of following the change management process for future requests to maintain control over scope changes.

4. If scope wasn't initially well-defined, work with the customer to clarify it.

5. If the customer is uncertain about their requirements, consider transitioning to an agile approach to refine the scope progressively.

Maintaining control over scope changes is crucial for project success. For practice, review a list of scope change requests for the hospital scheduling project and identify which ones fall outside the project's scope.

Monitor and control risks

Your risk management plan outlines the risks you're monitoring and the responses to address them. As the project advances, you must remain vigilant for these risks materializing, and if they do, swiftly execute the planned responses.

Each monitored risk in your risk management plan has an assigned owner responsible for continuous monitoring and status updates. Here's a detailed breakdown of what it means to own a risk:

1. Proactively implement risk responses before the risk materializes, taking preventive actions, mitigation measures, or contingency planning.

2. Keep a watchful eye on high-priority risks for any signs of unfolding events or triggers for contingency plans.

3. When a risk becomes reality, activate the pre-planned response and monitor its effectiveness.

4. Regularly report on risk status, updating the risk log and details sheet. Adjust risk probability or impact if circumstances change.

5. Consider closing risks that have become irrelevant as the project progresses. Review lower-priority risks periodically to reassess their significance and watch for new risks emerging due to project changes.

Effectively managing and controlling risks relies on having a well-structured plan in place. Practice by thinking about your response and rationale when a risk materializes.

How and when to use earned value analysis

Earned Value Analysis (EVA) is a project management technique used to assess project schedule and cost performance. It is particularly common in government projects. EVA is valuable because it provides insights that simple project metrics can overlook.

For instance, if 50% of the project's duration has passed and 50% of the budget has been spent, it might seem like everything is on track. However, if only 25% of the work is completed, there's a problem. You are now left with finishing 75% of the work with only 50% of the time and budget remaining, which may not be realistic.

EVA addresses such issues by assessing the project schedule and budget in monetary terms over time. It uses three key measures calculated up to the project status date:

1. Planned Value (Budgeted Cost of Work Scheduled): This is the planned expenditure to complete the scheduled work up to the status date. For example, if your baseline indicates $5,000 for a task through May 12th, that's the planned value.

2. Earned Value (Budgeted Cost of Work Performed): Earned value is the actual value derived from the completed work. For instance, if your team worked 30 hours by May 12th, with a planned labor cost of $3,000, your earned value is $3,000.

3. Actual Cost: This is the actual cost incurred for the completed work. If you ended up spending $3,500 for labor, that's your actual cost.

An EVA graph displays these values over time. Time is on the horizontal axis, while cost is on the vertical axis. Ideally, you want to see earned value exceeding planned value, indicating that you've completed more work than anticipated, signifying being ahead of schedule. Additionally, you want to see the actual cost below earned value, indicating that you've spent less on completed work than planned, implying being under budget.

Evaluate progress

During project execution, it's crucial to assess the project's status by examining both the schedule and costs. Begin by using a Gantt chart to compare the current schedule with your original baseline plan. By analyzing the task bars' positions and the time scale, you can determine whether tasks are ahead of, behind, or on schedule.

For instance, if the current task bars for implementation are scheduled later than the baseline, it indicates they are behind schedule. Variance values provide the specific difference between the baseline and current schedule. In the example, the finish variance is -25 days, indicating that you need to shorten the remaining schedule by 25 days to get back on track.

To address issues and maintain schedule adherence, focus on problematic tasks. Scheduling software often includes tools for early detection of delays, such as identifying incomplete tasks running behind schedule, tasks that should have commenced but haven't, or tasks where work hours lag behind schedule.

Additionally, it's essential to compare project costs to the budgeted values using cost variances. If the project is exceeding the budget, investigate the reasons behind it. Potential causes may include scope creep, where work was performed without additional budget allocation, or tasks taking longer than planned, leading to higher labor costs. Conversely, if work progresses more rapidly than expected, it can give the appearance of exceeding the budget, but this may normalize if the work aligns with your initial estimate.

Once you've assessed the project's status and identified problems, you'll have the information necessary to devise solutions.

How to get a project back on track

When your project encounters issues, it's essential to determine how to bring it back on task. The approach you select and the permissions you need depend on various factors. If your project is lagging behind schedule, you can explore methods like fast tracking, crashing, or implementing overtime to accelerate the project's completion. In cases of budget overruns, consider opting for more cost-effective resources or reducing other expenses. As a last resort, contemplate scope reduction, as it can both expedite the schedule and lower costs.

Start by implementing solutions that fall within your authorization, avoiding the need for permission to make changes. For instance, you can reassign tasks to expedite work or reduce costs without affecting external parties. These changes can be executed without requiring approval.

If a solution exceeds your authority, seek approval from your customer or stakeholders. Extending the schedule, increasing the budget, or reducing scope typically necessitates consent from the customer, sponsor, or management team. When requesting approval, present your recommendations, including the advantages and disadvantages of each, and be prepared to address inquiries regarding your proposed solution and the ones you discarded.

In cases where your organization manages numerous projects, you may need to engage parties beyond your project stakeholders. For example, if you require contingency funds or resources from other projects, you'll likely need to seek approval from the management team.

Even if you manage your projects effectively, occasional deviations from the plan are inevitable. Instead of panicking, assess your available options and request assistance thoughtfully. Choose an approach to expedite the remaining schedule and identify the appropriate party to seek permission from based on the provided background information.

Close a project

When your project's deliverables are finished, there are some essential activities to complete before considering the project concluded. The most crucial aspect of closure is obtaining the customer's agreement that the project has been successfully completed, ideally in written form. This is typically achieved through a meeting where the customer and stakeholders sign the acceptance form.

The next step in closing is to document the lessons learned during the project. This involves identifying what worked well, what didn't, and how processes can be improved. These insights can enhance the performance of future projects.

Additionally, you should generate final documentation and a closeout report summarizing the project's performance. Finally, it's time to wrap up contracts, archive project information, and transition your team to their next assignments.

How to obtain customer acceptance

The project isn't considered finished until the customer approves it, but this doesn't mean they can keep requesting additional work. During the closing phase, acceptance tests are conducted to demonstrate the project's completion. In the planning phase, project deliverables and clear, measurable success criteria were defined. Now, acceptance tests are designed to verify whether the deliverables meet these criteria. Procedures for conducting these tests are also documented.

For instance, in the case of the hospital scheduling project, initial acceptance tests may focus on system functionality and device connectivity. Subsequent tests may assess data upload accuracy and the efficiency of common scheduling tasks. Once all acceptance tests are completed, a brief sign-off meeting is held with the customer and key stakeholders to obtain their agreement that the deliverables are complete and successful. This milestone is significant and warrants celebration.

As practice, consider identifying existing project documents that can be used to create acceptance tests for the hospital scheduling project.

Document lessons learned

In every project, there are successes and areas for improvement. Don't let this valuable experience go to waste. Collecting lessons learned allows you to replicate your achievements and enhance areas where performance fell short. Let's explore ways to extract this information from your team members and document these lessons for the benefit of future projects.

First, make it a regular practice to schedule time for lessons learned discussions. Don't wait until the project's end, as team members tend to forget important insights by then. One approach is to include lessons learned as a topic in your ongoing status meetings. Ensure that your lessons learned sessions maintain a positive and productive atmosphere. Start by discussing what went well. Ask each team member for tips or techniques that improved their work, such as time-saving strategies or how they successfully tackled challenging problems. Then, shift the focus to lessons learned from encountered issues. Maintain a positive tone by asking what they would do differently next time. Encourage team members to share their experiences rather than assigning blame to others.

Create an environment where people can be open and honest. Consider scheduling meetings without managers to foster more open information sharing. To address sensitive topics or situations where individuals may be hesitant to admit mistakes, implement an anonymous method for submitting lessons learned, such as a suggestion box.

Finally, ensure that lessons learned are documented. You can add them to your project notebook and also establish a knowledge base, like a webpage featuring frequently asked questions. This allows everyone in your organization to benefit from the knowledge your team has accumulated. Lessons learned provide an opportunity for your organization to learn and grow with each new project.

As practice, develop a plan for sharing lessons learned among schedulers and IT teams in the consortium, assuming they share a collaboration system.

How to prepare a close-out report

In every project, there are successes and areas for improvement. Don't let this valuable experience go to waste. Collecting lessons learned allows you to replicate your achievements and enhance areas where performance fell short. Let's explore ways to extract this information from your team members and document these lessons for the benefit of future projects.

First, make it a regular practice to schedule time for lessons learned discussions. Don't wait until the project's end, as team members tend to forget important insights by then. One approach is to include lessons learned as a topic in your ongoing status meetings. Ensure that your lessons learned sessions maintain a positive and productive atmosphere. Start by discussing what went well. Ask each team member for tips or techniques that improved their work, such as time-saving strategies or how they successfully tackled challenging problems. Then, shift the focus to lessons learned from encountered issues. Maintain a positive tone by asking what they would do differently next time. Encourage team members to share their experiences rather than assigning blame to others.

Create an environment where people can be open and honest. Consider scheduling meetings without managers to foster more open information sharing. To address sensitive topics or situations where individuals may be hesitant to admit mistakes, implement an anonymous method for submitting lessons learned, such as a suggestion box.

Finally, ensure that lessons learned are documented. You can add them to your project notebook and also establish a knowledge base, like a webpage featuring frequently asked questions. This allows everyone in your organization to benefit from the knowledge your team has accumulated. Lessons learned provide an opportunity for your organization to learn and grow with each new project.

As practice, develop a plan for sharing lessons learned among schedulers and IT teams in the consortium, assuming they share a collaboration system.

Learn how to close and transition projects

As your project nears its conclusion, there are essential loose ends to address. Firstly, ensure the closure of any contracts you've entered into. If your project involved a customer contract, their signed acceptance indicates their satisfaction. Depending on contract terms, you may have additional obligations such as post-project support or follow-ups.

Once the scheduling system is operational, assess its performance against hospital objectives and verify vendor contract compliance before closing them. If another group assumes responsibility post-project, ensure they are prepared for the transition as the project integrates into daily operations. This involves helping your team transition to their new roles.

Archiving project information electronically facilitates retrieval and sharing. Depending on your company's technology, you can store project files on a network drive, in a database, or a document management system.

Finally, close the accounts used for billing project costs, typically leaving them open for a few months for follow-up expenses like support. With these tasks completed, your project is officially finished, and your role as project manager concludes. Take a moment to celebrate your achievements before moving on to your next project.

Create organizational value through a value delivery system

Organizations don't embark on projects just for the sake of it; they do so to attain value. The Project Management Body of Knowledge's seventh edition introduces a value delivery system to emphasize this pursuit of value and offer a high-level mechanism to achieve it. Value can manifest in various ways. For instance, Bryceland Hospital aims to enhance operations to reduce costs and enhance healthcare quality, as seen in our example project. This project will provide value by implementing a new scheduling system and engaging in process improvements to meet these objectives. Suppose the hospital's CEO also desires to boost patient ratings, ultimately increasing market share. To achieve this, the hospital could consider a set of patient-centric projects aimed at enhancing customer satisfaction.

Now, let's explore the value delivery system outlined in the PMI's project management standard. While junior project managers might not directly contribute to building such a system, understanding how project-related efforts contribute value to organizations can be beneficial. The value delivery system commences with an organization's senior leadership, who have a vision for the organization and formulate a strategy and plan to realize that vision. In our Bryceland Hospital example, the COO envisions improving operations to cut costs and enhance healthcare, while the CEO aspires for Bryceland to become the preferred hospital in the area. They adopt strategies like employing technology and process improvements for operational enhancement and implementing web-based services to enhance patient satisfaction. Leadership identifies the desired outcomes based on these strategies, which can be tangible, such as products or services for hospital patients, or indirect, like improved customer satisfaction through process enhancements.

These strategies drive the portfolios that the organization initiates. Within a portfolio, there may be individual projects and programs consisting of multiple projects. For instance, Bryceland Hospital may create one portfolio for endeavors related to operational enhancement and another for website and app services. The operational improvement portfolio could include our scheduling project and possibly other projects focused on different operational aspects like billing.

However, the value delivery system isn't complete without a mechanism to ensure that value is genuinely realized. When projects conclude and outcomes are delivered, leadership can evaluate the achieved outcomes, benefits, and value against their expectations. Depending on the value realized, they may adjust their strategies, which, in turn, might lead to modifications or additions to portfolios, programs, and projects. There's a feedback loop in this system as well. Operations can provide feedback to program and project teams regarding fixes and other changes that could enhance value. Program and project teams report performance and progress information up to the portfolio level, and portfolio managers convey overall portfolio performance to the leadership team. This illustrates how a value delivery system can assist an organization in deriving value from project-related endeavors.

Principle-based project management

PMBOK 7 presents 12 guiding principles for effective project management. These principles offer direction for decision-making, problem-solving, and strategy development in projects. Here's a brief overview:

1. Caring Stewards: Project managers act as diligent stewards who deeply care about project outcomes, including financial, social, technical, and environmental impacts.

2. Engaged and Empowered Teams: Successful projects thrive when teams collaborate effectively, and project managers play a crucial role in fostering a supportive team environment.

3. Value Delivery: Project managers prioritize delivering value throughout a project's life by continuously evaluating outcomes and adapting plans to maximize value.

4. Holistic Perspective: Projects are complex systems with interconnected components, and teams must consider both internal and external factors to achieve positive outcomes.

5. Tailored Approach: Rather than adhering to a rigid methodology, teams should choose the right approach based on specific project requirements, focusing on value, cost management, and efficiency.

6. Quality: Quality is ensured by meeting stakeholders' expectations and acceptance criteria through processes like testing, reviews, and error identification.

7. Adaptive Practices: Recognizing that complexity and change are inherent in projects, teams should build adaptability and resilience into their approach.

8. Positive and Negative Risks: Teams should leverage positive risks (opportunities) while mitigating negative risks (threats) to achieve project objectives.

9. Change and Challenge: Projects inherently bring about change, requiring organizational change management to transition stakeholders from the current state to the future state.

Applying these principles can contribute to successful project outcomes for all involved.

Focus on project outcomes through performance domains

PMBOK 7 outlines eight performance domains, which guide activities for achieving desired project outcomes and value. These domains emphasize delivering outcomes, benefits, and value and replace the knowledge areas from previous editions.

1. Stakeholder Engagement: Focuses on tasks to ensure stakeholder satisfaction by identifying, analyzing, and engaging with project stakeholders.

2. High-Performance Teams: Encourages effective teamwork and leadership within the project team, fostering a culture of collaboration and excellence.

3. Development Approach and Life Cycle: Tailors the project's development approach and life cycle to the type of deliverables, considering single or periodic deliveries, using predictive or adaptive methods.

4. Planning for Outcomes: Emphasizes outcome-driven project planning, ensuring appropriate planning efforts while allowing for adjustments as needed.

5. Project Work: Involves activities to maintain focus, efficient work processes, resource management, and procurement, if necessary.

6. Delivery Assurance: Ensures project deliverables align with requirements, scope, and quality expectations, supporting business objectives.

7. Measurement: Involves tracking progress and performance and making necessary development corrections to keep the project on track.

8. Uncertainty Management: Addresses the identification, assessment, and handling of project risks, both threats and opportunities.

These domains collectively ensure that projects successfully deliver desired outcomes, benefits, and value.

Tailor your approach to meet project and organizational needs

Project management isn't one-size-fits-all; it needs customization. Factors like project size, duration, complexity, industry, and organizational culture influence tailoring. You must balance effective management with avoiding unnecessary processes. Consider the project's lifecycle and approach, like Agile or waterfall. Processes can be adjusted for regulatory requirements or team performance. Tailoring applies to team composition and empowerment levels. Integrating internal and external resources is crucial. Software and hardware should align with your project's needs, especially in Agile. Adapt methods, documents, templates, and artifacts as required for an effective project environment.

Models, methods, and artifacts

In PMBOK 7, the section on models, methods, and artifacts offers a resource of tools, techniques, and outputs for project management. Unlike previous editions, PMBOK 7 provides a menu of options without strict prescriptions. Models simplify real-world concepts; for instance, it includes communication models for different contexts and models for organizational change and team development. Methods are approaches to achieve specific outcomes, like estimation, data analysis, and meeting facilitation, among others. Artifacts encompass documents, templates, or project deliverables, including business cases, project charters, and various plans. This section helps project managers choose suitable tools for effective project management.

Next steps

As a project manager, you'll have a dynamic and highly sought-after role. Your newfound skills may even improve your productivity in various aspects of life. With these foundational principles, you're well-prepared to initiate, plan, manage, control, and successfully conclude projects. Remember to celebrate your achievements along the way.

Whether you're starting your journey or refreshing your skills, numerous additional resources are available to support your growth. To learn more or pursue certification, visit the PMI or PRINCE2 websites.

Chapter 2 Project Management Ethics

Overview: Project ethical values

As project managers, we encounter numerous ethical dilemmas in our roles, which involve reshaping our organizations, collaborating with diverse individuals, and overseeing procurement activities. The Project Management Institute (PMI) offers a Code of Ethics and Professional Conduct to guide us in making ethical choices, based on four core values: responsibility, respect, fairness, and honesty.

Responsibility, as defined by PMI, entails owning our decisions, actions, and their consequences. As project managers, this extends to our discussions, relationships, and all means we employ to achieve project goals.

Respect, according to PMI, involves holding ourselves, others, and entrusted resources in high regard. These resources encompass people, finances, reputation, safety, and environmental assets, making us stewards of our businesses.

Fairness, as per PMI, means making impartial and objective decisions, free from self-interest, prejudice, or favoritism. It is particularly relevant in procurement processes, where personal relationships with vendors can compromise fairness.

Honesty, as defined by PMI, requires understanding and conveying the truth in both communication and conduct. Every communication we share should lead to a truthful perception, ensuring transparency and integrity.

By embracing these principles, you can confidently face your reflection in the mirror each morning.

Demonstrating responsibility

Being accountable and demonstrating ownership are essential aspects of showcasing responsibility as a project manager. It's likely that your boss recognized these qualities when selecting you for the role. However, even highly responsible individuals can encounter challenges in project management. To steer clear of these pitfalls, adhere to these guiding principles:

1. Focus on managing rather than assigning blame. Project managers often have limited control over the outcome, as tasks assigned may not always be completed on time or to the desired standard. Taking responsibility means proactively managing the situation rather than pointing fingers. Keep in close communication with your team, ensuring they have the necessary information and tools for successful task completion.

2. Adapt your plans instead of lamenting reality. Despite meticulous planning, numerous factors can disrupt your project. When priorities shift or unforeseen business or technical issues arise, acknowledge them, assess their impact, and adjust your plans accordingly.

3. Respond to project challenges in support of your team. While it can be tempting for project managers to step in and complete tasks when the project

falls behind, doing so may inadvertently convey a lack of trust in your team's abilities or raise technical concerns. Instead, offer support in a collaborative manner, ensuring your actions align with your team's work and maintaining open communication.

4. Collaborate with your boss and prioritize the interests of the business. Consider ethical dilemmas, such as launching a project without a business case when instructed by your manager. While this situation may raise concerns, your manager may have the authority to proceed. In such cases, proceed but express the importance of sharing expectations for project benefits and costs as soon as possible. However, never fabricate data for a business case, as it compromises your integrity and can lead to unforeseen questions.

By adhering to these principles, you will continue to meet the expectations of the boss who chose you as a project manager due to your responsible conduct, ensuring they are never disappointed.

Displaying respect in project management

Stewardship, a word I cherish, encapsulates the responsibility of overseeing and guiding a project towards achieving the value outlined in the business case. As project stewards, we manage the finances spent, our sponsors' resources utilized for project delivery, and the project as a whole. Beyond these tangible aspects, my focus lies on demonstrating respect in project delivery:

1. Time is a precious resource, and once lost, it cannot be recovered. As project managers, we must be mindful of both our own and our stakeholders' time. Treasuring their time demonstrates a heightened level of respect.

2. Brainpower is another resource deserving of respect. A respectful project manager simplifies decision-making for their superiors by framing questions clearly, providing pros and cons for informed decisions, and offering advance notice of significant decisions to allow stakeholders to prepare.

3. The emotional well-being of your team is crucial. Technical challenges and tight deadlines can induce stress. Care for your team by assessing their stress levels and shielding them from additional stressors whenever possible.

4. Demonstrating respect involves advocating for the ethics of your business and key stakeholders. While often straightforward, situations like conflicting directives from senior stakeholders may arise. Smartly, evaluate the corporate

procedures and your own ethical principles. If needed, engage in transparent discussions with stakeholders to seek alignment and avoid misunderstandings.

Respecting your business, project, stakeholders, and yourself is a foundational aspect of ethical behavior that should guide your daily actions as a project manager.

Operate with fairness

Of PMI's four ethical values, fairness resonates with me the most. Childhood memories of modifying neighborhood games to ensure fairness still stand out. Fairness is not only crucial in our roles as project managers but also as individuals. To maintain a reputation of fairness, focus on these four key aspects:

1. Abstain when in doubt: Refrain from making decisions if there's any uncertainty about your ability to remain fair and impartial.

2. Balance workload: Strive to distribute work equitably among team members, avoiding favoritism or overburdening certain individuals.

3. Be fair to yourself: Acknowledge your own limitations and competencies, ensuring you don't take on tasks beyond your expertise.

4. Evaluate based on performance: When assessing team members, prioritize objective performance evaluations over personal preferences.

Consider John, a project manager who exemplifies fairness. He abstained from evaluating a vendor with whom he had a prior connection, ensuring impartiality. During a staffing challenge, John distributed work evenly, offering opportunities for all team members to contribute and learn. He didn't overload himself, recognizing his own limitations. When evaluating a team member, John prioritized performance feedback over personal liking.

Emulate John's fairness, and your project management endeavors will be characterized by equity and harmony.

Behaving with honesty

For instance, Jane's project management role reinforces her reputation for honesty through her daily actions:

1. Clear Communication: Jane prioritizes project-related communications that educate and enhance understanding. Her meetings focus on providing direction and insights into the project's trajectory, backed by facts and intuition to predict future developments and their impact on the business.

2. Effective Status Reports: Jane considers status reports as powerful tools for stakeholder management. She ensures they offer a comprehensive view of the project's status, fostering transparency and clarity.

3. Predictability: Jane strives to be predictable in her interactions with sponsors and stakeholders. By proactively planning and sharing her approaches and consistently following through, she builds trust and promotes honesty.

4. Timely Sharing of Information: Jane understands the importance of sharing project updates promptly, including bad news. Instead of concealing issues while attempting to resolve them, she believes in addressing concerns immediately, enhancing her reputation as an honest project manager.

5. Transparency: Transparency is a key facet of Jane's approach. She believes in sharing information generously, even beyond what is strictly necessary for the task at hand. Her willingness to be forthright, as demonstrated when recruiting a contractor, fosters trust and builds strong professional relationships.

Emulating Jane's commitment to transparency, timely communication, predictability, and knowledge sharing can elevate your standing as a project manager known for honesty and integrity.

Mandatory ethics

In project management, we often refer to rules, norms, and guidelines. Rules are strict behaviors to always follow, norms are generally expected behaviors, and guidelines allow flexibility in specific situations. The Project Management Institute (PMI) defines mandatory standards as firm requirements, akin to rules. Violating these ethical standards can jeopardize your PMI membership. Examples include negotiating in good faith (respect) and avoiding dishonest behavior for personal gain (honesty). While these standards may seem common sense, they're vital, especially in complex projects. Here's how I leverage them: I share expenditure details openly with sponsors, emphasizing transparency and respect. When making recommendations, I present both project and business perspectives, fostering fairness and responsibility. These standards aren't constraints; they're tools for project management success.

Aspirational ethics

PMI defines aspirational standards as conduct we strive to uphold as professionals, even if they aren't easily measured. These standards are not optional. They allow project managers to apply ethics contextually. Let's discuss a couple of examples:

1. Responsibility: The standard states, "We accept only assignments consistent with our background, experience, skills, and qualifications." This emphasizes alignment with your background. While it's valuable to stretch your skills, there's a reasonability test. Assess if you genuinely believe you can handle a role before applying.

2. Respect: The standard suggests, "We approach directly those with whom we have a conflict." Address disagreements with direct communication to find common ground. However, some situations may be impractical for direct confrontation. In such cases, work within the boundaries of integrity and practicality.

Applying aspirational standards involves interpreting PMI's ethical values. It's about embracing their intent and using available resources to uphold ethical behavior. This approach not only benefits project delivery but also guides life's ethical choices.

Establishing personal ethical standards

Effective ethical standards depend on our thought processes and responses to challenges. Crafting your ethical code based on your character, experience, and culture serves as your best guide to ethical behavior. Let's see how Marie, a thoughtful project manager, applies the four ethical values:

1. Responsibility: Marie extends her care beyond her project to her team, investing time to share experiences and even delegate tasks. This investment enhances her team's skills and project integrity.

2. Respect: Marie treats all stakeholders, including supporters, opponents, and skeptics, with equal attention. Her openness and communication earn respect, even if she doesn't win everyone over.

3. Fairness: Marie practices what she preaches, never asking her team to do something she wouldn't do herself. She evaluates outcomes over techniques and ensures her team has the necessary tools and support.

4. Honesty: Marie's honesty shines through in how she delivers challenging news. She believes in the power of truth, knowing that people can handle it, and she actively works to address issues.

By adhering to her personal ethical standards, Marie enjoys trust from stakeholders and loyalty from her team. Similarly, you can build trust and loyalty by holding yourself accountable for your ethical conduct.

Ethics in initiation and planning

Project initiation is an exciting phase where project scope and objectives take shape, but it can also generate anxiety. It's crucial to uphold ethical integrity during this stage. Here are key ethical considerations:

1. Transparency in Business Case Development: Be completely transparent when justifying project savings or revenue increases in your business case. Ensure all data supporting your claims is captured and defensible. Avoid overstatements.

2. Explicitly State Assumptions: In the early project stages, acknowledge that some information may be based on assumptions rather than facts. Clearly label and communicate these assumptions until they can be validated.

3. Appropriate Estimation Labels: Use estimation labels (e.g., order of magnitude, budgetary, definitive) to indicate the level of certainty in your estimates. Avoid providing estimates that suggest more data or knowledge than you possess.

4. Formal Project Approval: Avoid prematurely conveying that the project will proceed, even if you receive positive signals from sponsors. Wait for formal organizational approval before informing team members or vendors. Doing otherwise can lead to irreversible financial and emotional consequences for stakeholders.

Prioritizing ethics during initiation sets the stage for ethical expectations throughout the project lifecycle.

Ethics in procurement and contracting

Project procurement and contracting ethics receive significant attention due to the substantial investments involved in responding to requests and potential contract revenue. To ensure equitable treatment, project managers must maintain consistency and prevent bias in their decision-making. Here are common pitfalls to avoid:

1. Transparent Vendor Relationships: Disclose current, past, and perceived vendor relationships to prevent bias perceptions. Clarity in these relationships is crucial to maintain fairness.

2. Bias Recognition: Acknowledge any biases you may have based on technical or business experience. Objectivity is vital, regardless of personal preferences or unconscious biases.

3. Predefined Evaluation Process: Develop a vendor and solution evaluation process in advance. Define your business needs and create a scoring mechanism to assess solutions objectively. This preparation reduces the risk of favoring one vendor or solution.

4. Prioritize Critical Criteria: Avoid evaluating noncritical elements with the same weight as vital business conditions. Assess proposals based on the criteria that truly matter for your business, ensuring fair and meaningful evaluations.

By navigating these pitfalls and prioritizing ethical considerations, you can maintain fairness and integrity in project procurement and contracting.

Ethics in execution and closure

While this might not seem like an optimistic way to begin, it's essential to recognize that not everything in your project plans will unfold as envisioned. Ethical communication is paramount during project execution. Here are key tips:

1. Clear and Timely Status Reports: Ensure your status reports are clear, concise, and issued on schedule. Avoid delaying reports in the hope of resolving issues before reporting them. Your sponsor needs a full and timely understanding of the project's status.

2. Adherence to Standards: Deliver project products according to predetermined standards and avoid cutting corners, even when facing challenges. These standards were established for a reason, and compromising them without stakeholder agreement is not ethical. Strive to provide an acceptable product.

3. Accountability and Responsibility: Share responsibility when things are going well, but remember that, as the leader, you're accountable when things go

awry. Accepting accountability, rather than blaming the team, is essential for ethical standing. Embrace failures as opportunities for learning and improvement.

By embracing failure as a stepping stone and practicing ethical communication and accountability, you can maintain your ethical integrity during project execution.

Reporting ethical problems

We've explored the Project Management Institute (PMI) Code of Ethics, with a particular focus on the ethical value of responsibility. One crucial aspect of responsibility outlined by PMI pertains to reporting ethical standards violations. I'd like to emphasize two key points from this mandatory standard:

1. Reporting Unethical or Illegal Conduct: We are obligated to report any unethical or illegal behavior to the appropriate management and, if necessary, to those affected by the conduct.

2. Substantiated Ethics Complaints: Ethics complaints should only be filed when they are supported by verifiable facts.

While this reporting duty may be viewed negatively as 'snitching,' I believe it is a means to protect others from harm caused by unethical behavior. If we're aware of someone being harmed and do nothing, we indirectly contribute to that harm. Here's how I approach this reporting process:

1. Ensure Claims Are Fact-Based: Always substantiate your claims with factual, firsthand information.

2. Involve Affected Parties: Whenever possible, involve those affected by the unethical behavior. Sharing indisputable facts with them can help rectify or prevent unjust outcomes and garner additional support for your cause.

3. Stick to the Facts: When reporting to management, present the facts without jumping to conclusions.

4. Consider Alternative Reporting Channels: If you believe that management is involved in the unethical behavior, explore other internal avenues for reporting, such as Human Resources or Corporate Affairs.

It's important to acknowledge that reporting unethical behavior can sometimes lead to negative consequences, including potential backlash. Therefore, involving affected parties early on can serve as a protective measure and enhance the credibility of your ethics report. While this topic may not be pleasant, it is of utmost importance. As project managers, we bear the responsibility of safeguarding our stakeholders, and when we can prevent harm, it becomes our ethical duty to do so with fairness and integrity.

Ethical decision steps

Ethical standards alone are just one piece of the puzzle; the other crucial part is having a practical, repeatable approach to ethical decision-making. To assist project managers in this endeavor, PMI has introduced an ethical decision-making framework, comprising a series of sequential steps.

1. Gather All Relevant Information: Start by ensuring you have a comprehensive understanding of the ethical dilemma. This includes specifics about the incident, applicable legal and ethical standards, your personal ethical beliefs, and relevant cultural norms.

2. Explore Your Choices: Delve into the available options for addressing the issue. Create a list of pros and cons for each option you consider.

3. Choose the Best Solution: When making your choice, be in the right mental state. Emotional influences can cloud judgment, so ensure your decision is not unduly influenced by external factors. Ask yourself if the chosen option will still seem wise a year from now.

4. Apply Ethical Principles: Evaluate your decision in light of ethical principles. Consider whether it promotes the greater good and is fair to all parties involved.

5. Make Your Decision: If you are willing to openly share your decision, along with the rationale behind it, and take full responsibility for the outcomes, you're ready to proceed.

While the ethical decision-making framework may appear straightforward, it becomes invaluable when faced with challenging ethical dilemmas. I recommend keeping this framework handy to ensure your ethical decisions are thorough and characterized by integrity.

Alternatives and analysis activities

To effectively evaluate ethical alternatives, I rely on a question-based approach that helps uncover nuanced perspectives and alternative solutions. Here are key questions I consider:

1. Can We Explore Alternatives Beyond A or B? Avoid limiting choices to a simple A versus B scenario. Consider whether a combination of A plus additional actions or B plus additional actions could provide a more suitable solution. Flexibility in options can alleviate ethical dilemmas.

2. Is Compassion a Relevant Factor? Compassion plays a role in ethical evaluations. Two cases illustrate this: one where an individual showed no remorse for misusing funds and another where remorse and attempts to rectify the situation were evident. Understanding the motivations behind ethical compromises can highlight the importance of compassion in decision-making.

3. What Was the Intent Behind the Ethical Violation? Intent matters. In one instance, a colleague broke a rule to benefit a client by sharing unreleased product details. Understanding the intention behind ethical breaches can guide ethical evaluations.

Managing ethics involves exploring questions and considering contextual factors. Incorporate these questions into your ethical discussions to expand your decision-making options.

Application and action activities

Following the ethical analysis, I take some final steps before acting. I mentally prepare by envisioning explaining my decision to my mother, which serves as a gut check to ensure I'm making the right choice. This approach helps me keep my explanations concise and focused on essential facts.

Regarding intuition, I compare it to the known facts and logic of my decision. If there's misalignment, I seek input from others to refine the solution.

For executing ethical decisions, I recommend creating a communication plan, considering who needs to be informed and in what order. Starting with your manager or sponsor is often a good choice. Be decisive in your actions and avoid public self-doubt, as this can create unnecessary uncertainty among your team members. If you're confident in your decision, proceed with it.

Next steps

Successfully managing ethics on projects offers significant benefits. As you tackle larger and more ambitious projects, the likelihood of encountering ethical challenges increases. Your overall project success can hinge on your ability to recognize and address ethical issues. I recommend reviewing the complete PMI code of ethics and professional conduct, along with the PMI ethical decision-making framework. Additionally, consider reading Ralph Kleim's book 'Ethics and Project Management,' which delves deeper into the concepts. Remember, your mirror is the best judge of your actions. By embracing these principles and being honest with yourself, you're more likely to consistently make ethical choices.

Chapter 3 Project Management Requirements

Manage project requirements challenges

Effective requirements management is crucial for project success. While specific details and terminology vary by industry, the overarching challenges remain consistent. It boils down to answering four essential questions from project initiation to completion, accounting for potential changes.

1. Who are our stakeholders? Stakeholders are those whose satisfaction impacts the project's outcome.

2. What are their precise wants and needs? These are the project's requirements, and they must be clearly articulated and documented.

3. How important are each of these requirements? Prioritization helps when resources are limited.

4. How will we handle conflicts, changes, surprises, and miscommunications as the project unfolds?

To address these challenges effectively, I follow a 10-step requirements management process, which we'll cover in this book. In any project, our team's goal is to deliver a working solution that satisfies customers and meets business needs. Our team's success hinges on how well we manage project requirements.

Identify standards

When dealing with complex projects, it's crucial to gather extensive information without overlooking any details. It greatly benefits the entire team if everyone follows a consistent approach to requirement management. Some industries have established formal standards to provide a shared framework. Here are three examples:

1. The International Standards Organization (ISO) offers ISO 21500, Guidance on Project Management, which outlines how projects, including requirement management, should be handled. This standard aligns with the Project Management Body of Knowledge (PMBOK) from the Project Management Institute (PMI).

2. Software developers and those in the electronics industry can refer to a joint standard from ISO, IEC, and IEEE, titled 29148-2018 International Standard for Systems and Software Engineering Life Cycle Processes - Requirements Engineering. Access may be possible through a subscription to the Standards library or by purchasing it from the IEEE website.

3. Companies involved in the defense industry should be acquainted with military specifications (MilSpecs). The U.S. military standard for project management is MIL-STD-961E, Defense and Program-Unique Specifications Format and Content, available for free from the Defense Logistics Agency website.

Additionally, it's essential to be familiar with a common technique of gathering stakeholders in workshops to establish project requirements. These workshops may be known as Requirements Discovery and Analysis Workshops, Joint Application Design (JAD), Joint Requirements Planning (JRP), or Joint Application Requirements (JAR). Using formal standards or recognized techniques can minimize confusion, enhance team collaboration, and may even be required by customers. Knowing which standards apply to your industry and company is the first step in effective project requirement management.

Prepare the elicitation plan

Michelangelo stated, "Every block of stone has a statue inside it, and it's the task of the sculptor to discover it," aligns with our goal in eliciting project requirements. Just as hidden statues are within stone, project requirements are concealed within stakeholders and businesses. Our role is to uncover these requirements. We achieve this by creating a requirements elicitation plan, which essentially means gathering data.

The plan outlines the information we aim to collect and how we'll obtain it. Methods for eliciting requirements include interviews with stakeholders, group sessions, observing work processes, and analyzing business data. The plan should specify who to involve and what questions to ask, ensuring we identify project requirements accurately.

Regardless of the elicitation techniques you employ, it's essential to document them in your plan and review it to ensure you're addressing the right questions and sources to define project requirements effectively.

Identify the stakeholders

Every individual or group impacted by a project is a stakeholder. To capture project requirements effectively, we must identify and analyze these stakeholders. Start by creating a stakeholder list, which can include names, roles, or groups. For instance, list your project sponsor and customers collectively instead of naming each customer.

After listing stakeholders, it's crucial to understand their project relationship. Determine if they advocate for or oppose the project. Assess their influence on a scale of one to ten, with ten being critical support. Rate them based on the project's impact on their work or life, with ten indicating significant change.

Stakeholder analysis serves three purposes: it ensures consideration of all stakeholders and their project impact, aids in developing a comprehensive requirement elicitation plan, and assists in creating a communication strategy to engage and inform stakeholders throughout the project.

Stakeholder analysis helps comprehend how your project affects individuals and ensures project success.

Gather project requirements

Our goal is to uncover hidden requirements and bring them to light. To do this effectively, we must align our data gathering methods with information sources.

For input from senior executives, schedule one-on-one meetings, explain the project, and ask open-ended questions like, "What defines project success?" For input from a larger customer base, consider using online surveys, such as Qualtrics or Survey Monkey, which offer free versions and templates.

Here are four helpful tips:

1. Capture stakeholders' input verbatim to avoid bias.

2. If unclear, ask follow-up questions until understanding is clear.

3. Maintain thorough notes and summarize requirements in a matrix.

4. Be adaptable and ready to adjust your approach as new stakeholders and insights emerge, gradually revealing the project's needs for success.

Analyze requirements

As project managers, organization is crucial, especially when gathering requirements. We must also document attributes for each requirement to create a structured foundation for our project. You can aligning with the business analysis body of knowledge, which focuses on these 10 attributes:

1. Absolute reference: A unique identification number for the requirement.

2. Complexity: The difficulty level of addressing the requirement, often rated on a scale or categorized as easy, medium, or hard.

3. Risk: The level of uncertainty associated with the requirement.

4. Author: The person who documented or elicited the requirement.

5. Source: The origin of the requirement's information.

6. Ownership: The individual responsible for addressing the requirement.

7. Stability: Whether the requirement is well-defined or may require modification.

8. Urgency: Whether the requirement requires immediate attention or can wait.

9. Priority: The importance of the requirement in the context of the entire project.

10. State: The current status of the requirement, whether it's in draft form or fully documented and approved.

You may not need all these attributes or may discover others essential to your project. The key is that documenting attributes helps you organize and manage requirements, ensuring your project aligns with stakeholder needs and expectations.

Prioritize project requirements

Prioritizing project requirements can be challenging. While elicitation may generate numerous requirements, the project can't accommodate them all. To address this, we use the attributes and stakeholder analysis we've collected:

1. Identify conflicts among requirements, resolving differences between stakeholders' needs, even if it means compromise.

2. Ensure uniqueness of requirements by eliminating duplicates or combining similar ones.

3. Simplify complex requirements by breaking them into smaller, manageable parts.

4. Evaluate requirement importance; for smaller projects, categorize as necessary or optional, while larger projects can rank on a scale of one to 10.

Determining priority depends on the project, involving either team consensus or decisions made by the project sponsor or product manager. Documenting requirement priorities and tracking changes is crucial. Prioritizing helps in defining project scope and allocating resources effectively, recognizing that not all requests can be accommodated.

Create use cases

Project requirements detail stakeholders' desires for a solution but often lack the context needed for effective solution development. We can address this issue by using requirements to create use cases. A use case narrates how a solution should function, offering a step-by-step account of a process and the actions or events required. A single use case can support multiple requirements. Key terms include "actors" for the people and systems involved in a use case and "actions" or "events" for the steps.

For instance, let's create a use case for ordering pizza at a restaurant with actors like the customer, waiter, chef, and computer. The process involves the waiter taking the order, entering it into the computer, transmitting it to the chef, and serving the pizza to the customer.

Use cases can be communicated through written descriptions or visual diagrams like swim lane diagrams or Unified Modeling Language (UML) for more complex processes, particularly in software development. Proper use of use cases adds context to requirements, facilitating collaboration and the creation of better solutions.

Document project requirements

To shape a project using the information collected from stakeholders, we create a requirements report, also known as a scope document. Think of this report as a narrative explaining the project's purpose and significance. It typically includes:

1. An executive summary.

2. Background information explaining the project's business importance and stakeholders.

3. Sections on project goals, scope (inclusions and exclusions), anticipated risks, and interdependencies with other projects.

4. A glossary for technical projects to define key terms.

5. Detailed but not overly technical requirements that focus on what needs to be achieved, not how.

When documenting requirements, ensure they meet three criteria: clarity and specificity, thoroughness (including source and importance), and testability. Regularly update the report and establish version control to maintain accuracy and alignment with project goals. The requirements report serves as the foundation for the entire project, making effective documentation crucial for team success.

Approve project requirements

To transition from information gathering to project work, we must obtain approval for our requirements. This approval process involves two steps:

1. Stakeholder Review: Initially, we offer stakeholders the opportunity to review our documentation to ensure the accuracy of their requirements. This step might be challenging, as stakeholders are busy and may question the need for a second review. However, it allows them to grasp the full project requirements and provide any final input before management approval.

2. Management Approval: After stakeholder reviews, we deliver the finalized requirements report. Approval procedures can vary between organizations,

ranging from formal stage gates to informal methods like email or meetings with the project sponsor. Ideally, if you followed the requirements development process correctly, approval should be straightforward. However, questions or concerns may arise, necessitating revisions and reiterations until all approvers are in agreement.

Obtaining requirements approval is a significant project milestone, offering an opportunity to acknowledge the contributions of stakeholders and team members while instilling confidence that everyone is aligned with the project's objectives.

Manage change requirements

Change is a constant in projects, even after requirements are approved. We must be prepared for this inevitability. Reasons for changes include missed requirements, evolving project insights, or shifts in the business environment. To manage these changes effectively, implement a versioning process:

1. Change Requests: Establish a process for submitting, reviewing, and approving change requests. A change request template can ensure essential details are provided, such as the nature of the change, the requester, and its significance. Notify requesters if a change is not approved.

2. Incorporating Changes: When a change is approved, incorporate it into the requirements report, creating a new version. Maintain a revision number and include a change log in the report, summarizing each revision and the approval date.

3. Document Accessibility: Ensure that everyone working with the requirements report uses the most current version. This is straightforward with electronic documents, but communicate changes effectively through your communications plan, specifying who needs to be informed and how.

Flexible requirements allow projects to align with evolving business needs. Being ready for changes and having a well-managed process in place enhances adaptability and agility across all project aspects.

Manage the project requirements process

Project requirements form the essential foundation for every project. They bridge the gap between business needs, customer requirements, and the tasks undertaken by project teams. Project Managers and Business Analysts hold vital roles in ensuring well-defined and well-managed requirements. This book has guided you through a 10-step process for effective requirements management. While not all projects may require all 10 steps, having them in your toolkit ensures a comprehensive approach.

Chapter 4 Project Management Schedules

Why do you need a schedule?

Managing project schedules is akin to cooking. You gather ingredients (project details), create the schedule "recipe," adjust the elements for the right balance, and then continually monitor and adjust as needed until the project is done. A project schedule is crucial because it ensures that all necessary work is completed as planned.

Imagine a busy day with a to-do list—you prioritize tasks for efficient completion. Similarly, a project schedule organizes all project work, assigns responsibilities, and defines the sequence of tasks. It also serves as a communication tool, showing how project components interconnect. This helps team members collaborate effectively and informs stakeholders about progress.

Moreover, a schedule makes work clear and manageable for team members, enabling them to understand their tasks and deadlines. Project managers can use it to track progress and make adjustments as the project evolves, guiding it towards success.

Schedules within the project life cycle

Managing a project schedule is an ongoing process, not a one-time task. In the Project Management Book of Knowledge (PMBOK), it falls under the Project Schedule Management knowledge area. In earlier editions, it was referred to as Time Management.

Here's an overview of the project schedule life cycle:

1. Planning: Determine how you'll schedule the project, choose scheduling tools, and decide on the measurement units (e.g., hours, days, weeks). This plan can be formal or informal, depending on your project.

2. Activity Definition: Define project activities or tasks, starting with the project scope and work breakdown structure (WBS). Work packages within the WBS

break down into activities, specifying what needs to be done for each deliverable.

3. Sequencing: Arrange activities in a logical sequence based on dependencies or relationships. For example, Activity A must finish before Activity B can start. This establishes the order of work.

4. Resource Estimation: Estimate the resources required for each activity, including people, equipment, and materials. These estimates help determine activity durations and costs.

5. Scheduling: Develop the schedule using various techniques (e.g., critical path method, critical chain method, Scrum, Kanban). It often takes multiple iterations to create a realistic schedule. The final result is the baseline schedule, representing the target delivery.

6. Monitoring and Controlling: Once the project starts, continuously monitor progress against the baseline schedule. If deviations occur, take corrective action to realign the project.

7. Closing: After project completion, compare the original schedule with the actual outcomes to refine future project estimates and schedules.

Remember, managing a project schedule is an ongoing effort, adapting as needed throughout the project's life cycle.

Develop a schedule management plan

Creating a schedule management plan might seem excessive, but it's simply about documenting the scheduling decisions you make for your project. Whether it's formal or informal depends on your project's needs. Here's what it involves:

1. Method Choice: Select the scheduling method, like critical path method, critical chain, Scrum, or Kanban. Consider any approved methods your organization may already have. In this book, we'll focus on the critical path method.

2. Tool Selection: Choose a scheduling tool that aligns with your selected method, such as Primavera or Microsoft Project.

3. Accuracy and Measurement: Decide how accurate you want your estimates to be (e.g., plus or minus 50%, 25%, or 10%). Determine whether you'll measure work effort in hours, days, or weeks. For our example, we aim for plus or minus 10% accuracy and mostly use days for tasks.

4. Update Procedures: Describe how you'll gather data from the team, update your schedule, and specify the update frequency. In our example, weekly updates are reported regarding task start dates, days worked, and estimated remaining days.

5. Corrective Action: Define the variance from the baseline schedule that triggers corrective action. In our example, action is taken if a task is delayed by a week.

For larger projects, you may document more detailed processes and performance measures for consistent execution. Developing a step-by-step schedule management plan ensures consistency. For practice, create a schedule management plan for one of your projects.

Determine the level of detail in your schedule

The level of detail in your project schedule depends on the project's size and your team's experience. Here's how to approach it:

1. Summary Schedule: For large or complex projects, consider having schedules at different levels of detail. A summary schedule provides a high-level overview, highlighting key milestones and major deliverables. It's perfect for conveying the big picture to management and those not needing intricate details.

2. Intermediate Level Schedule: This level includes all milestones and deliverables, breaking down the work to the level of work packages. A work package represents the effort needed for a project deliverable. It provides a comprehensive view of the project without delving into the activities required to complete a work package.

3. Detailed Schedule: The most detailed schedule includes milestones, deliverables, and all the activities necessary to complete work packages. For smaller projects, one detailed schedule may suffice. As you learn more about the project, refine your schedule, starting with rough estimates and progressively adding more accurate details.

4. Breaking Down Large Projects: With large projects, consider creating multiple detailed schedules, each focusing on a major deliverable (e.g., training guide and website in our example). If contractors or vendors are involved, integrate their schedules into the overall project schedule to cover all project activities.

5. Use Project Management Software: Most project management tools allow you to link detailed schedules to a higher-level schedule, providing flexibility to view the project from various angles.

Tailor your schedules to match your project's needs for control and effective communication with stakeholders and team members.

Identify project activities

Efficient project management relies on thorough work identification and appropriate granularity. This covers tasks performed by both internal resources and external parties. Here's a concise breakdown of the process:

1. Work Breakdown Structure (WBS): Initiate work identification through a WBS when defining project scope. Start with a list of high-level deliverables, named using nouns (e.g., "published training guide" and "launched website").

2. Lower-Level Deliverables: Identify sub-deliverables beneath the high-level ones, such as "completed manuscript," "laid out training guide," and "training guide available for sale." These are known as work packages. Ensure activities unrelated to deliverables, like project management, supervision, reporting, and communication, are included.

3. Activity Identification: Determine the specific activities required to complete each work package. These activities are named using verb-noun combinations. For instance, the work package "revised manuscript" may involve activities like "review manuscript for technical accuracy" and "correct manuscript." Assign a unique identifier, like a WBS code, to each activity for easy tracking and association with project documentation.

4. Appropriate Sizing: Ensure activities are of suitable size for estimation, assignment, and tracking, typically falling within the range of eight to 80 hours or one to 10 workdays. For larger projects, consider sizing activities between 20 to 80 hours to maintain a manageable activity list.

5. Evaluation Methods: Assess activity size based on the required accuracy for time and cost estimation. Break down activities until you achieve the needed

precision. Additionally, consider whether activities can be assigned to individuals or small teams, align with reporting periods, and possess distinct beginnings and ends for straightforward status tracking.

6. Team Collaboration: In larger projects, involve a small planning team to break down the initial deliverable levels. Assign sections to different teams for further detailing of work packages and activities. Consolidate all activities into the overall project schedule, eliminating any duplicate entries.

By following these steps, you can efficiently identify and structure project work, ensuring smoother project execution.

Add milestones to your schedule

Milestones are pivotal markers in your schedule for tracking progress and flagging significant events. They don't involve effort, thus having no impact on project duration or labor hours. Here's a concise guide on their strategic placement:

1. Project Start and Finish: Include milestones at the project's beginning and end. The start milestone indicates when the project commences, and if the start date shifts, the milestone moves accordingly. The end milestone signifies when all project scope must conclude, offering insights into project schedule performance.

2. Phase Start and End: For project phases, add milestones at their beginning and end. This allows for adjustments if preceding activities encounter delays, influencing subsequent phases. It's wise to place an additional milestone at the conclusion of each phase.

3. Deliverable Completion: Create milestones to mark the completion of deliverables, each with well-defined criteria for validation. Naming them with the deliverable name and status ensures clarity. For instance, "Manuscript Complete" and "Layout Verified."

4. Decision Points: Use milestones to signal significant decisions or review points, indicating whether the project should proceed. If decision-making is postponed, rescheduling the milestone will automatically adjust subsequent activities.

5. Handoffs to Teams: Employ milestones to denote handoffs to other teams, helping teams anticipate when their involvement begins.

6. Key Events: Flag essential occurrences like printer deliveries with milestones.

Milestones are an efficient way to visually communicate progress to stakeholders, providing an instant overview of project status. Their advantage lies in their non-disruptive nature, allowing you to add as many as needed without affecting project duration. When there are extended intervals between milestones, consider adding more to highlight progress during each reporting period. Milestones serve as valuable tools for tracking progress, decision points, handovers, and crucial events, enriching project management without affecting project timelines.

Organize project work

You can organize project activities in three main ways: by deliverable, phase, or group. The choice or combination depends on your project planning and management approach.

1. By Deliverable: Arrange activities based on the specific deliverables they contribute to. This method aligns with a structured breakdown of deliverables in your work breakdown structure (WBS).

2. By Phase: Organize work according to distinct project phases, such as design, development, and production. This approach is suitable if your project involves go/no-go decisions at phase boundaries. For instance, you might group activities for a feasibility study within a phase.

3. By Group: If different teams or departments handle separate aspects of the project, consider organizing work by these groups. This method is beneficial when various teams collaborate, and it facilitates understanding each team's contribution to the project.

In practice, you can even combine these methods to suit your project's unique needs. There's no one-size-fits-all approach; choose the organization method that aligns best with your project management goals for a successful outcome. You can experiment with these methods on your own projects to find the most effective approach.

Estimate duration and work

Estimating activity effort is crucial for scheduling. Here's an approach to make estimating easier:

1. Rolling Wave Planning: Begin with a rough estimate (±50%) to evaluate project feasibility. Gradually refine estimates to ±25% for mid-range accuracy. Detailed estimates (±10%) take more time but are close to final figures.

2. Duration vs. Work Hours: Decide whether to estimate in duration (e.g., 8 days) or work hours (e.g., 60 hours per chapter). Detailed work-hour estimates can lead to more accuracy.

3. Clarify Assumptions: When using duration estimates, clarify assumptions with estimators (e.g., full-time or part-time work). With work-hour estimates, you can derive duration based on available resources (e.g., 8 days for one writer or 4 days for two writers).

Estimates are essential for predicting project duration and costs.

Methods for estimating activities

Estimating duration and work involves various methods tailored to your project's needs, organization's practices, available historical data, and resources. Here are some effective approaches:

1. Use Historical Data: If available, rely on past project data or team performance to derive accurate estimates.

2. Expert Estimates: Engage individuals familiar with the work, like team members or external consultants. Provide them with project details and activities to estimate.

3. Delphi Method: Seek estimates from multiple experts independently. Share and ask for re-estimates several times, using the average of the final round as your estimate.

4. PERT (Program Evaluation and Review Technique): Request optimistic, pessimistic, and most likely estimates for tasks. Use these to calculate a weighted average and run simulations to assess project outcomes and probabilities.

5. Industry-Specific Methods: Depending on your industry, there may be specialized estimation techniques to explore.

Remember to adapt your estimation approach to the unique characteristics of your project and seek input from colleagues for additional insights.

Put activities in order

Sequencing work correctly is vital. Imagine constructing a skyscraper's penthouse before its foundation; it wouldn't make sense. Activity sequencing predicts when work happens and how the schedule reacts to resource changes, delays, or scope adjustments. Activities influence each other through links or dependencies, which can be visualized in network diagrams or Gantt charts.

Network diagrams display activities in boxes connected by arrows, while Gantt charts list activities on the left with scheduled timelines on the right, linked by arrows indicating dependencies. To identify dependencies, consider which activity initiates the sequence. The triggering activity is the predecessor, and the one it triggers is the successor. Determine whether the predecessor's start or finish date initiates the second activity, forming the dependency type.

Finish-to-start dependencies, where the first activity's finish date triggers the second's start date, are most common. For instance, creating an outline must finish before building a template can start. Finish-to-finish dependencies occur when one activity's finish date controls another's finish. Start-to-start and start-to-finish dependencies exist but are less common. Understanding these links shapes your project schedule.

Handle lag in dependencies

Sometimes, there's a delay between activities, meaning the successor doesn't commence right after the predecessor concludes. For instance, reviewing the manuscript can't finish immediately after writing it; there's a delay while reviewers assess the final chapters. You can model such delays by adding "lag" to the task dependency, which most scheduling tools support.

For instance, if reviewers need five days after receiving the last chapters to complete their review, you add a five-day lag to the link, scheduling the review to finish five days after the manuscript. Lag can also represent non-work-related delays, like concrete curing time. Always provide a note explaining the reason for any lag you add. When lag involves effort, you can reflect it by creating a new activity, like "print training guides," and linking it to milestones to track progress. Avoid using lag as buffers for risk events, and never use negative lag (lead) between activities, as it can lead to scheduling issues. Lag has its place in scheduling, but it's not frequently needed.

Problems with start-to-start dependencies

Start-to-start dependencies indicate that one activity's commencement dictates when another activity starts. A common scheduling error is connecting activities with a start-to-start dependency when a finish-to-finish relationship should be used. This can lead to issues, as illustrated in the writing and reviewing manuscript example. Each task takes 10 days, and when linked with a start-to-start relationship and a two-day lag, problems arise if the writing takes longer than expected, such as 15 days. In this scenario, the reviewing task is still scheduled to finish on the 12th day, two days after it starts and with a 10-day duration, which is before the writing is completed. This means some pages may go unreviewed or reviewers must wait. In this example, a finish-to-finish dependency is more appropriate because reviewing should finish when writing finishes. Start-to-start dependencies are suitable when activities must commence simultaneously, like leveling concrete shortly after pouring it, before it hardens. To avoid link issues, it's essential to determine whether the predecessor's start or finish controls the successor.

Best practices for sequencing activities

A well-structured schedule offers a realistic timeline for activities and should be adaptable to changes during project execution. The sequencing of activities, which determines schedule logic, is crucial. Follow these best practices for activity sequencing:

1. Primarily use finish-to-start dependencies.

2. Minimize start-to-start links, reserving them for specific cases where necessary.

3. Use start-to-finish links sparingly, only if truly required.

4. Apply lag to represent the passage of time, not delays caused by work.

5. Avoid negative lag or lead; consider shorter tasks with finish-to-start links instead.

6. Ensure each activity, except the first and last, has at least one predecessor and one successor.

7. Don't link summary tasks, as they summarize their constituent activities.

8. Eliminate redundant and circular links for clear schedule logic.

9. Use date constraints only when absolutely necessary, as they limit schedule flexibility.

10. After sequencing activities, review and adjust schedule logic based on these guidelines.

Plan resources at a high level

Your schedule must encompass all necessary project resources. A resource plan, also known as a staffing plan, facilitates the allocation of required resources in line with project needs. To create a resource plan, identify necessary skills, as well as materials, equipment, facilities, and travel. Utilize a spreadsheet, listing resources in the first column and time periods (e.g., weeks or months) across the rest of the columns. Populate cells at the intersection of time and resource with quantities required during those periods.

Labor is often measured in hours or full-time equivalents (FTEs), with one FTE representing a full-time worker. Another approach involves using a scheduling program, setting up generic resources for identified skills and other resources, and assigning them to project activities.

A resource plan aids in determining the quantity and procurement of resources. Review the plan for potential shortages, adjust activity durations if needed, consider internal or external resource options, and work backward from resource availability to procurement timing. Update the plan as commitments for resources become available, providing a high-level view of resource needs for developing a realistic project schedule.

Procure resources

Resource availability and skill levels significantly impact your schedule. Acquiring the right resources for your project is a valuable skill. How you secure resources depends on their source and your organization's procurement processes. If new to procurement, consult HR, managers, or experienced project managers to estimate process duration and factor it into your schedule.

For in-house staffing, identify existing procurement processes in small organizations or secure commitments from managers in larger ones. As the project start nears, finalize commitments by selecting individuals with the required skills and experience.

When obtaining external resources, additional steps like bidding, vendor selection, and contract signing may be necessary. Preferred vendors with standing contracts can expedite this process. Establish relationships with resource managers and potential team members to improve your chances of securing top resources.

Understanding your organization's processes, planning for procurement lead time, and fostering relationships will help you acquire the best resources for your project.

Define resources in your schedule

Once you've identified the necessary resources, it's time to incorporate them into your schedule. How you define these resources depends on the scheduling software you're using.

1. Labor Resources: These are tracked by the time they contribute to the project. Specify their availability (full-time, half-time) and hourly rates, including overtime if applicable.

2. Equipment and Facilities: If they are assigned by time (e.g., a crane at $500 per day or office space at $5,000 per month), set them up as work resources. Create calendars to specify their availability and calculate costs based on usage duration.

3. Material Resources: Tracked by quantity, specify how many you need and their cost per unit (e.g., computers, construction materials like cubic yards of concrete).

4. Non-work Resources: Include resources like building permits, travel expenses, or fixed-price subcontracts by specifying their cost. If quantity is needed, set it to one.

After defining resource availability, quantities, and costs, you can assign them to specific project activities.

Balance resource assignment variables

Resource assignments involve three key factors: duration, work (effort), and resource availability (units), which can be adjusted to meet scheduling goals or address scheduling challenges. Duration refers to the activity's time from start to finish, while work represents the hours required to complete it. Resource availability, or units, signifies the time allocated for someone to work on the activity. These three variables are related by the equation: Duration = Work / Resource Units. You can modify any two of these variables but not all three.

To illustrate, consider an activity with an estimated eight hours of work. If the assigned person is available full time, the activity will take eight hours, resulting in a duration of one work day. Typically, an activity's work remains constant, leaving you with two scenarios: Set the duration if you know how long you want the activity to take, determining the required resource units for that duration. Alternatively, assign resource units if you know the resource availability, with the duration based on work and units. These three variables offer flexibility when assigning resources to activities.

Keep an assignment variable fixed

Scheduling tools offer flexibility in choosing whether to keep duration, work, or resource units constant when adjusting resource assignments.

1. Keeping Work Fixed: This option is practical when you estimate work for project activities. You add resources and their availability to the project, and the tool calculates the duration based on the assigned work. Changing resource units will adjust duration while keeping work constant, and altering the duration will recalculate resource units needed to complete the task.

2. Keeping Duration Fixed: This is useful when you either don't assign resources to activities or must complete activities within a specified timeframe. Fixed duration allows for precise duration settings, such as whole or half days, and ensures the duration remains unchanged, even if you modify assignments. The tool calculates resource units based on the specified work.

3. Keeping Resource Units Fixed: Although less commonly used in organizations, this option is suitable when resource availability remains fixed. It's particularly helpful for individual workload management. The tool calculates duration based on estimated work, and any changes in work adjust the duration. For strict deadlines, you can override resource units to maintain the duration.

Select the fixed variable based on your project scheduling needs. Some tools also offer features to designate activities as fixed duration or variable duration (effort-driven scheduling), where total work remains constant regardless of resource assignment modifications. Make your choice based on project requirements.

Assign resources to activities

Resource assignments play a crucial role in project scheduling because they impact activity duration and timing. In many cases, team members are not identified until later in the planning process, leading to initial scheduling based on estimates of resource availability and expertise.

If the team is not yet established, generic resources can represent required roles or skills. Resources should be assigned to work package activities, the lowest level tasks, as these represent the actual work. Summary activities and milestones should not have resources assigned to them.

When estimating work, assign the expected number of resources, and the scheduling tool will calculate activity duration. Conversely, if you estimate duration and assign available resources, the tool calculates the work they can accomplish in that timeframe.

Ensure all necessary resources, including materials, equipment, and ancillary costs like travel, are assigned to activities. This comprehensive approach allows you to determine the project's schedule and total cost.

Replace generic resources with people

When you learn the identities of your project team members, you can replace generic resources with individuals. However, remember that the assumptions made during estimation carry inherent risks. These assumptions may not align with reality, such as resource availability, skill levels, or their familiarity with your organization.

Before substituting generic resources with specific individuals, you require three key pieces of information:

1. The resource managers' input on experience and productivity levels.

2. Knowledge of their availability for your project.

3. An understanding of their time commitment, whether full-time or part-time.

With this information, you can adjust or create resource assignments to reflect actual conditions. For example, if two experienced writers are assigned but one is unavailable until May 1st, replace the generic resources with only one writer for the initial writing activity, altering the duration accordingly.

In cases where a team member proves to be less productive than anticipated, you can increase work hours for the activity to accommodate the extended timeframe. For instance, if a new team member like Jane requires extra time to get up to speed, adjust the work hours accordingly.

If team members do not directly report their time into your scheduling system, keeping generic assignments can be an option for easier resource allocation. However, this approach may lead to a less precise schedule and challenges in progress tracking. Conversely, assigning specific individuals to activities allows for accurate scheduling and tracking, ensuring precise assignment and allocation management.

Working with part-time workers and teams

Accurate assignment of part-time workers and teams is vital for precise project schedule forecasting. When assigning a part-time worker, start by defining their project availability. Adjust the assignment to reflect their part-time status and consider specifying their work hours when necessary.

For activities requiring collaboration, schedule work during the part-timer's available hours, ensuring alignment with their schedule. Alternatively, inquire if the part-time worker can adjust their availability to match the activity schedule, especially when multiple participants can meet at the same time.

When assigning a team with identical skills, use the team's name rather than individual names. Team availability often exceeds full-time, such as 200% for a two-person team. Calculate activity duration based on the team's collective work hours per week. Account for communication and interaction overhead by adding 5% to 10% to your work hour estimate when switching from an individual to a team assignment.

By aligning part-time worker and team assignments with their availability, you can construct a more precise schedule, facilitating better project management during execution.

Working with remote teams

When managing remote teams, scheduling requires careful consideration of their unique dynamics. Factoring in the advantages and disadvantages of remote work is crucial for maintaining project efficiency.

Begin by aligning remote team members' work schedules with their respective working days and times. If dealing with different time zones, select a primary time zone for the project and establish each individual's working hours based on that zone. Be mindful of holidays and non-working periods that may vary among team members from different companies or countries.

International teams can extend your project's effective work hours, allowing for tasks to flow seamlessly between time zones. However, remember to account for coordination, communication, and potential misunderstandings by adding 5% to 10% to your estimates.

Remote teams also offer the advantage of increased resources for activities, potentially expediting task completion. Keep in mind that distance can sometimes hinder productivity and effective communication. To address this, promote team building through conference calls or video meetings, hold regular online updates, improve phone and email communication, and provide diversity training to enhance collaboration across cultures.

Understanding how remote teams function enables you to optimize the benefits and mitigate challenges in your project schedule.

What is the critical path?

The critical path is the longest sequence of activities in a project from start to finish. It's crucial because changes in critical path activity dates impact the project's finish date. If critical activities are delayed, the whole project is delayed, and if they finish early, the project finishes early. Critical path tasks share the characteristic of having zero total float, meaning they cannot be delayed without affecting the project's finish date. Understanding and managing the critical path is essential for on-time project delivery or schedule compression if necessary.

Determine the critical path

Understanding the critical path involves calculating activity dates and total float to identify critical activities. Total float represents the time an activity can be delayed without affecting the project finish date. It's calculated by subtracting early finish from late finish or early start from late start.

To calculate total float, you perform a forward pass to determine early start and early finish and a backward pass to find late start and late finish. The difference between early and late start or early and late finish yields the total float for each activity.

Activities with zero total float are on the critical path and cannot be delayed without affecting the project's finish date. Activities with positive total float can be delayed by that amount without impacting the project's finish date.

Understanding the critical path enables you to make schedule adjustments or shorten the project as needed.

Put the critical path to work

To maintain or expedite your project's schedule, it's essential to manage activities on the critical path. Critical activities hold the key to shortening the project timeline while ensuring realistic adjustments. Focus on the critical path, as indicated by red bars in our example, to keep the project on task. This approach is particularly helpful when your project faces delays or requires an earlier finish date.

Start by shortening critical path activities, like assigning two proofreaders to reduce one week from the training guide schedule. However, be aware that modifying one activity on the critical path may alter the critical path itself, potentially making other activities critical. Therefore, always recalculate the path after adjustments and document the changes and reasons behind them to maintain clarity and project alignment.

By fine-tuning critical path activities, you can successfully manage your project's timeline or recover from delays.

Too many or too few critical tasks

Critical activities typically have no slack, but various factors in your schedule can affect slack calculations. Avoid using date constraints unless absolutely necessary, as they can limit schedule flexibility and influence total slack calculations.

For instance, if a project manager imposes a "finish no later than" constraint on the project's completion milestone, it may cause several tasks to finish later than the milestone, resulting in negative total slack. This can lead to an excessive number of activities marked as critical in your schedule, making it challenging to identify genuinely critical tasks.

To address this issue, focus on activities with the smallest slack values, even if they are negative, such as -10 days. If possible, adjust the critical threshold setting in your scheduling program to the lowest total slack value in your schedule, like -10 days. This adjustment will designate activities with slack greater than -10 days as non-critical.

In cases where there are gaps in your schedule's critical path, review activity dependencies, ensure clear schedule logic, and be cautious with date constraints. Resource availability can also cause critical path gaps. Analyze whether these gaps are appropriate and genuine or if they can be resolved by finding alternative resources.

To identify critical activities, look for those with the least total slack, often referred to as the smallest "float." Adjust your scheduling program's critical activity threshold to match the smallest total slack value in your schedule for a more accurate critical path representation. These techniques can help you rectify critical path issues if your schedule contains an excessive or insufficient number of critical activities.

Lengthen, delay, or split assignments

After assigning individuals to tasks, it's essential to maintain a consistent workload for them. A balanced workload enhances efficiency and productivity. You can achieve this by employing three primary methods: extending, postponing, and splitting assignments.

1. Extending Assignments: This method is useful when someone is overwhelmed with concurrent tasks. You can increase the duration of assignments, allowing the person to work fewer hours on each task per day. For instance, if a graphic designer has two one-week tasks simultaneously, extending their duration to two weeks enables them to allocate time more effectively.

2. Postponing Assignments: Delays are effective for managing workloads, particularly when assignments are short. Delaying tasks helps individuals maintain focus and productivity. Generally, it's recommended not to juggle more than three assignments simultaneously. To alleviate workload, you can schedule assignments sequentially rather than concurrently.

3. Splitting Assignments: When you need to accommodate a brief but crucial task within a longer assignment, splitting the longer task into sections is a viable solution. For instance, if a writer has a five-week assignment but needs to

complete a two-day review, you can split the task to accommodate both the review and the writing.

When implementing workload management strategies, ensure that you document your decisions and solutions to provide clarity on the rationale behind your scheduling choices. Utilize these methods individually or in combination to optimize your project schedule for effectiveness and realism.

Adjust the level of work over time

Adapting work patterns over time can balance workloads and enhance schedule accuracy. Initially, when you assign individuals to tasks, work typically progresses at full capacity from start to finish. However, workloads can fluctuate during an assignment's duration.

Work contours, like bell curves or late peaks, illustrate these variations. Some scheduling programs allow you to apply these contours to activities to match individuals' changing work levels. If someone's work hours fluctuate day by day, choose a contour that mirrors these variations for the activity.

If you're uncertain about which contour to use for a particular project, seek advice from experienced project managers or team members. Keep in mind that not every activity requires a work contour. With more experience, you'll become better at determining when and how to use them.

While a work contour may extend the duration of an activity, it enables individuals to shift their focus between tasks, maintaining overall productivity. Work contours offer a more realistic representation of how work unfolds, contributing to improved workload balancing.

Replace overallocated resources

An effective way to balance workloads is by reassigning tasks to individuals who have more available time. This approach not only resolves overallocations but can also expedite the schedule, provided you have qualified replacements accessible.

Start by identifying team members who are overallocated on the project, such as the graphic designer handling both screenshots and illustrations simultaneously. Then, search for individuals possessing similar skills who can take on some of the overallocated work. Depending on project constraints, you can consider internal staff, contractors, or external vendors.

Once you've identified suitable replacements with availability, initiate the procurement process promptly. After securing replacements, adjust your schedule to reallocate the overallocated work. Ensure that the affected resource is aware of the assistance provided.

While this approach generally maintains the project's original timeline, there are considerations to bear in mind when procuring replacements. Replacements may be less experienced, potentially leading to longer completion times, lower quality, or a reliance on the existing team. Skilled replacements might come at a higher cost. Evaluate these factors and weigh them against the project's needs.

For example, if Jane is overloaded with her initial writing assignment, you can search for another writer or someone who can provide assistance. In this case, no additional writers are available, but you find an intern who can handle certain tasks. Reassigning work to others is an effective way to balance workloads, often without extending the schedule, provided you have access to additional resources with the required skills.

Include schedule contingency time

Schedule contingency serves as a safety net for on-time project delivery. Estimates inherently carry uncertainty, hinging on assumptions about various factors like resource availability and productivity. Unforeseen risks or issues can also impact project timelines, such as adverse weather delaying a construction project.

Avoid incorporating contingency time into individual work package activities, as it complicates management and needlessly extends the schedule. Instead, introduce separate contingency activities for specific reasons, like adapting to new technology or onboarding new team members. These contingency activities provide clear rationale and transparency, assuring stakeholders that the schedule isn't merely padded.

For instance, if management desires a 90% probability of finishing on or ahead of schedule, use statistical analysis to determine the halfway point between the most likely and worst-case durations. If the most likely duration is 30 weeks and the pessimistic estimate is 36 weeks, the 90% probability of on-time completion is 33 weeks.

To establish contingency, begin by adding a buffer activity at the end of each sequence of activities, enabling shared buffers for all activities within that sequence. Additionally, place buffers at the end of each major phase or section to address schedule risks resulting from converging paths. Finally, include one last buffer at the project's conclusion.

This approach allows you to monitor the project without immediate intervention at the first sign of trouble. You allocate buffer time to activities facing delays as needed, gradually taking action as buffer utilization reaches predetermined thresholds. By implementing contingency in this manner, your project is better equipped to maintain its on-time completion prospects.

Baseline the schedule

Once stakeholders approve the project plan, it's crucial to save it as the baseline, serving as the benchmark for comparing actual progress against the initial plan. Anything included in the baseline should be subject to the change control process. Any alterations made to the baseline are documented as change requests.

For different types of files like specifications or requirements, store the original versions in a designated baseline folder. When changes are necessary, edit a copy of the baseline document and mark revisions as change requests.

For project schedules, most scheduling software includes a baseline-saving feature. When you save a baseline this way, the program preserves the approved values such as start and finish dates, task duration, work hours, and costs. The value of saving a baseline becomes evident as you track progress or make schedule adjustments. You can compare planned values to current ones, looking for discrepancies in dates and costs.

For instance, if an activity takes longer than planned, it delays subsequent activities, and the start variance quantifies this delay. Visual cues like Gantt charts can display planned (gray) versus actual (blue) work periods, making it easy to spot delays or cost increases compared to the baseline, prompting corrective actions to realign the project.

Proactively manage a schedule

Project management involves maintaining a balance among scope, time, cost, resources, and quality. The adjustments you make to the schedule depend on stakeholders' priorities, which we'll delve into later in this chapter. Since schedule changes can bring about risks, you must also consider the level of risk that stakeholders are willing to tolerate.

Time frequently plays a pivotal role, whether it's ensuring a product launch aligns with peak sales season or outpacing market competition. During project execution, you keep an eye out for schedule issues. If delays threaten the project's finish date, you can employ strategies like fast tracking and crashing to expedite the remaining schedule.

If cost outweighs time in importance, there are ways to modify the schedule to reduce expenses. You may opt for more economical resources, even if they extend the timeline, or condense the schedule to trim overhead costs. When the project's finish date, budget, and resource constraints are non-negotiable, scope reduction becomes an option. This approach can expedite the schedule and lower costs, provided you trim less critical components while still delivering most of the intended benefits.

It's advisable to preserve quality as is since compromising it can lead to issues requiring time and money for resolution, negating any anticipated savings. Balancing project variables is an ongoing task throughout the project's lifecycle.

Update progress in the schedule

Projects rarely unfold exactly as planned, necessitating regular updates to your schedule to reflect actual progress. There's no universal method for collecting status information from teams, so let's explore effective approaches for updating progress. This will allow you to assess and, if needed, refine your organization's updating processes.

First, it's crucial to determine the optimal update frequency. Frequent updates can lead to excessive time spent on reporting progress, while infrequent updates may result in delayed issue resolution. The appropriate frequency depends on factors such as project duration, complexity, and risk. One strategy is to update your schedule more frequently than you report status to management. For instance, if you provide status reports every two weeks, consider updating progress on a weekly basis to proactively address issues. Always specify the status date for each update to distinguish between actual and remaining work.

You must also decide whether to use duration or work to record progress, then stick to your choice. Keep in mind that duration is easier to update but offers less accuracy. For each activity, gather the following information: activity name or ID, actual start date (if in progress), estimated start date (if not started), actual finish date (if completed), actual duration or work completed, and estimated remaining duration or work to get a comprehensive view of progress.

After recording an update, ensure the schedule's integrity. Completed activities should have actual start and finish dates earlier than the status date, while in-progress activities should feature actual start dates and actual duration or work completed before the status date. Unfinished work should be scheduled after the status date. Also, include incomplete activities that should be scheduled after the status date. Review the schedule logic to validate dependencies and adjust them as necessary to align with the current work sequence. Sometimes work may occur in a different order than initially planned, necessitating dependency revisions.

Evaluate the update's impact on the schedule and formulate response plans for any issues that arise. Lastly, document the update by explaining alterations to schedule logic, critical dates, and the critical path. Assign a version number to the update for easy identification and archive all update data. Properly updating a schedule is essential for maintaining a clear understanding of project status and next steps.

Find schedule problems

While work is in progress, it's crucial to monitor for potential schedule issues and take action before they escalate. Start by identifying activities that are commencing later than initially planned. Activities that deviate from their scheduled start times are likely to encounter delays in completing their tasks. If the delayed activity isn't on the critical path, it might not immediately impact the project's finish date but should still be flagged for observation. If it's a critical path activity, consider strategies to get it back on track. Additionally, investigate the reasons behind the late start. If predecessors contributed to the delay, address the issue to prevent it from affecting subsequent activities.

For example, if the writers report that chapters are taking longer due to discrepancies in software functionality, you might assign an assistant to resolve these issues, ensuring the writers can continue without further delays.

Next, identify activities currently scheduled to finish later than planned. Late starts can be one of the causes for late finishes, so some of these activities may already be on your radar. To uncover such issues, compare the actual hours worked with the planned hours. If less work has been completed than expected, it could lead to delays. Investigate the reasons behind this shortfall and take steps to resolve them, such as streamlining or reallocating administrative duties.

Another concern is when work hours exceed the original estimates. For instance, if the estimated duration for a task was 160 hours but the team reports it will require 200 hours, this can potentially extend the activity's duration and affect subsequent tasks.

To preempt a common issue of team members not promptly reporting delays or increased workload needs, foster a culture of open communication. Encourage team members to communicate early about any issues they encounter rather than waiting until the last minute, ensuring timely intervention.

Monitoring for early warnings of schedule delays allows you to proactively address and mitigate potential issues, helping keep your project on track.

Fast-track to shorten a schedule

During a project's execution, you can expedite the schedule by applying a technique known as fast-tracking, which involves adjusting the usual sequence of dependent activities to accelerate their completion. This strategy focuses on overlapping activities that would typically follow a sequential order, allowing the second activity to start before the first one concludes. However, it's important to closely monitor the initial activity for any potential delays, as any setbacks in its completion will affect the subsequent activity.

Fast-tracking is particularly effective for activities situated on the critical path, as compressing the critical path leads to an overall reduction in the project's duration. For instance, if the production editor begins formatting chapters as the writers finish them, this fast-tracking approach can complete both tasks in nine weeks instead of the usual 12, ultimately resulting in a three-week project time savings.

Despite its benefits, fast-tracking introduces a degree of project risk, such as the possibility of layout revisions due to manuscript changes, as seen in our example. To maximize the benefits of fast-tracking while minimizing risks, opt for activities with lower inherent risks.

It's advisable to fast-track one pair of activities at a time since overlapping activities can alter the critical path. If further acceleration is needed, choose additional activities on the adjusted critical path. The reduction in schedule duration achieved through fast-tracking is equal to the duration of the overlaps between critical path activities. The key to successful fast-tracking lies in selecting activities with minimal associated risks.

Pay more to shorten a schedule

When prioritizing the project's completion date over budget constraints, a viable option for expediting the schedule is referred to as "crashing." The primary method for crashing involves allocating additional resources to an activity, which proves effective up to a certain threshold. Overloading with excessive resources can hinder progress as individuals begin to impede each other's work. Alternatives for crashing include offering overtime pay, expediting delivery by paying fees, or hiring individuals capable of completing tasks more swiftly.

Crashing is most applicable to critical path tasks since they directly influence the project's finish date. However, it should be approached judiciously due to the increased risk it may introduce, especially when involving unfamiliar workers. Hence, minimizing the number of tasks subjected to crashing is advisable. Crashing longer tasks can yield significant time savings, reducing the need to crash multiple tasks.

Once potential candidates for crashing are identified, assess them to determine which offer the most cost-effective means of reducing the project's duration. The key is to select tasks that provide the lowest cost per week of schedule reduction. In the sample project, for instance, stakeholders demand an expedited project finish by one week.

Begin by identifying the longest critical path tasks with durations exceeding one week. Next, evaluate each candidate's potential for shortening and the associated cost, ultimately calculating the cost per day of crashing. Sorting the candidates by cost per week allows you to choose the most cost-effective option. In this example, both editing tasks can reduce the schedule by one week each for a cost of $1,500, making it a favorable choice.

By crashing one of the editing tasks, the initial publication date for the training guide is moved up to September 4th from September 11th, incurring an additional expense of $1,500. If further schedule reduction is required, repeat the process, starting with a review of the critical path, as the next task to be crashed must also be on the critical path. When the project's completion date takes precedence over budget considerations, crashing tasks proves to be a valuable strategy for expediting the schedule.

Change the schedule to reduce cost

When prioritizing cost considerations over the project's finish date, there are strategies to potentially reduce expenses. Initially, explore the option of utilizing more economical resources. Ideally, these resources would maintain the same work duration, resulting in clear cost savings. However, it's often the case that budget-friendly resources may require more time to complete tasks. For instance, a writer charging $150 per hour completes a task in 20 hours, while another writer costs $100 per hour. If the cheaper writer can complete the project in under 30 hours, cost savings are achieved. Nonetheless, it's essential to recognize that cost-effective options may extend project timelines.

Another approach involves extending task durations to avoid incurring overtime costs. For example, if a writer is scheduled for 20 hours of overtime at a rate of $20 per hour, delaying the task's finish date to eliminate overtime results in a $400 reduction in activity costs. Conversely, shortening task durations may yield cost savings for projects with high overhead expenses, such as leased office spaces or expensive rented equipment. Experimentation with various scenarios is often required to identify schedule modifications that effectively reduce project costs.

Reduce scope

When both the project finish date and budget are fixed, modifying project scope becomes a viable option for achieving balance. Reducing scope entails trimming the activities associated with delivering that scope, thereby subtracting time and cost from the schedule. Fewer critical path tasks result in a shorter schedule, while reduced work hours lead to lower labor and overhead costs. Nevertheless, adjusting project scope should be a last-resort measure due to its close alignment with the project's goals and objectives.

In many cases, stakeholders determine which aspects of scope to trim. However, if stakeholders seek suggestions, revisiting the project objectives can help identify the least critical components. In our sample project, the training guide holds top priority, while the website isn't causing scheduling issues. Initially, it may not seem like scope reduction will expedite the schedule. However, reducing scope doesn't need to be drastic or permanent.

One approach is to divide the project into segments, akin to an agile project. The essential scope is delivered in the initial iteration, followed by subsequent rounds to complete the remaining scope. In our example, breaking the training guide into beginner and advanced sections accelerates the schedule. The beginner guide can be published shortly after the software release on July 6th, with the advanced guide following on August 11th. This division results in an almost one-month acceleration compared to working on the guide as a whole. The advantage of scope reduction is its potential to shorten the schedule and reduce costs, making it a prudent adjustment to consider after exhausting other options.

Improve schedules

You can enhance your schedule management through a few key practices:

1. Receive training in schedule building: Attending project management classes can equip you with the knowledge of scheduling best practices. This understanding enables you to create more adaptable and realistic schedules, simplifying project management from start to finish.

2. Implement quality reviews for schedules: You can either personally assess your schedules using a checklist or establish a review process within your organization. In the latter case, project managers can convene review meetings to evaluate each other's schedules for accuracy.

3. Institute progress data collection processes: Launch procedures for gathering precise progress data and then compare this information with planned values. Estimates become more reliable when rooted in historical performance.

4. Leverage project assistants for larger projects: For substantial projects, having a project assistant proves invaluable. They can handle tasks such as schedule creation and updates, allowing the project manager to concentrate on leadership, communication, and achieving business goals.

These practices can contribute significantly to improving your project schedules and overall project performance.

Next steps

We've delved deep into project scheduling, covering various aspects from creating a schedule management plan to updating progress and resolving schedule challenges. I trust you've made significant strides in mastering project scheduling, but remember that there's always more to discover in project management. The more you learn and apply, the smoother your project deliveries will become.

Additionally, the Project Management Institute (PMI), a non-profit organization dedicated to advancing the project management profession, offers certifications like the PMI Scheduling Professional credential, which requires specific experience hours, accredited training, and passing a certification exam. PMI also publishes a practice standard for scheduling that delves into scheduling in greater depth.

Chapter 5 Project Management Budgets

Budget estimating parameters

Assessing the accuracy of your budget is crucial, as others relying on it need to have a clear understanding. To address this, consider providing a range for your estimate. For instance, if you estimate the project at $10,000 and four months for completion, you can inform stakeholders that costs might fall within the range of $9,000 to $13,000, with the duration spanning three to five months.

But how do you determine this range? In the initial project stages, you typically have limited information, resulting in what's known as an "order of magnitude" estimate. Typically, for such estimates, actual costs or durations could vary by 75% higher or 25% lower than your estimate. To refine your estimates, consider factors like scope, requirements, resource availability, material costs, and risk mitigation expenses.

This leads to a "budgetary estimate" with an accuracy range of 25% higher or 15% lower than actuals. Even without prior project data, you can provide a budgetary estimate as you gather more project details, such as scope, materials, and risk mitigation.

The most precise estimate is the "definitive estimate," based on project data, resource availability, and a detailed design. The target range for this estimate is typically 10% higher or 5% lower than your initial estimate.

It's essential to document the assumptions underlying your estimate, like resource availability, project work hours, and informal material costs. As the project unfolds, validate these assumptions and update your estimates accordingly. In summary, when asked about budget accuracy, emphasize that it improves continuously as you gather more information.

Budget estimating parameters

Evaluating budget accuracy is essential, as it impacts stakeholders. To address this, consider offering a range for your estimate. For instance, if you estimate the project at $10,000 and four months for completion, you can inform stakeholders that costs might range from $9,000 to $13,000, with the duration spanning three to five months.

In the project's early stages, you have limited data for your estimate, often referred to as an "order of magnitude" estimate. Typically, for such estimates, actual costs or durations could vary by 75% higher or 25% lower than your estimate. To enhance accuracy, refine your estimates by clarifying scope, requirements, resource availability, material costs, and risk mitigation expenses. This leads to a "budgetary estimate" with an accuracy range of 25% higher or 15% lower than actuals.

Even without prior project data, you can provide a budgetary estimate as you gather more project details like scope requirements, updated materials, and risk mitigation costs. The most precise estimate, the "definitive estimate," should be based on project data, resource availability, and a detailed design. The target range for this estimate is typically 10% higher or 5% lower than your initial estimate.

Crucially, document assumptions for the estimate, such as resource availability, project work hours per team member, and unquoted material costs. As the project progresses, validate these assumptions and adjust your estimates accordingly. In summary, when asked about budget accuracy, emphasize its continuous improvement as you gather more information.

Budget variables in your budget

While the "less is more" philosophy can be effective for project deliverables, it takes a different approach when constructing a project budget. In this case, gathering extensive data is crucial. Here's my method for developing a robust project budget:

1. Begin by compiling project requirements and creating a documented Work Breakdown Structure (WBS), as defined by the Project Management Institute. The WBS breaks down the entire scope of work needed to achieve project objectives and produce required deliverables, serving as the budget's foundation.

2. Estimate the number of hours required for each activity listed in the WBS. Consider specifying skill levels, as different levels of expertise may impact the time needed. For instance, a senior-level person might require 30 hours, while a less experienced individual might need 40 hours for the same task. If multiple team members are involved, estimate hours for each.

3. Verify the unit cost per hour, which can significantly vary between consultants and internal employees.

4. In some cases, tasks may be duration-based rather than hours-based. For instance, it might take three weeks to purchase, configure, and install a machine, requiring only four labor hours. Ensure to account for both the duration and labor hours as needed.

5. Don't overlook miscellaneous costs, including project management time, travel expenses, team events, licenses, building leases, and tools necessary for project support.

6. Consider any physical resources required, such as equipment and materials. This encompasses hardware, software, raw materials, or any essentials for solution development. If obtaining materials involves a tender process, include activities related to the tender in your WBS.

Although this process demands effort, it results in a realistic and defensible budget that aligns with project goals. So, in contrast to "less is more," building a project budget adheres to the principle of "more is more." The more detailed your budget creation, the better the outcome.

Budget accuracy and precision

Managing a project budget is akin to a delicate balancing act. You need to stay informed without hovering over your team, causing undue stress. To achieve this balance, it's crucial to grasp the concepts of accuracy and precision in budget management.

Accuracy pertains to the correctness of an estimate, characterized by order of magnitude, budgetary, and definitive estimates. Early-stage estimates have a broad range (e.g., 75% higher to 25% lower), resulting in lower accuracy. As you gather more project data, the range tightens, increasing accuracy. Understand which costs are unknown and when they will become known, especially when tender processes are involved.

Precision, on the other hand, refers to the level of exactness associated with an estimate. For instance, estimating eight hours is more precise than stating "sometime this week." The level of precision should align with your project's needs. Projects with shorter timelines require higher precision, as there's less room for deviation. Longer projects can afford to be less precise.

Strike the right balance between staying informed about your budget and avoiding excessive micromanagement. This balance ensures your budget remains under control as you navigate the project management tightrope successfully.

Baselines and contingency for your budget

Just as speed limits keep us safe on the road, project baselines are essential for our project's safety. Once your budget is finalized and approved, it's time to establish a budget baseline. This baseline serves as a reference point for comparing predicted costs. According to PMI, a baseline is "the approved version of a work product used as a basis for comparison to actual results." As the project progresses, actual costs are measured against this agreed-upon baseline, allowing you to gauge whether you're over or under budget.

Having a baseline also enables you to make adjustments when stakeholders request changes to your project's scope. If such changes are approved, you modify the original baseline to account for the impacts on project costs or schedule.

Before gaining budget approval, consider establishing a contingency reserve, defined by PMI as "time or money allocated in the schedule or cost baseline for known risks with active response strategies." You can determine the required contingency reserve by assessing the project's risk factor. For instance, a low-risk project might allocate an additional 5% to the contingency reserve, while a high-risk project may need 20%. The risk level serves as your guide for determining the necessary contingency.

It's crucial to keep the contingency reserve separate from the original budget. When reporting project progress, use the $100,000 budget figure and treat the $10,000 contingency reserve as if it doesn't exist, unless needed. Project baselines and contingency reserves, like speed limits, are necessary to ensure safe project navigation towards successful outcomes.

Forecasting and building a budget

Operating without a project budget is akin to shopping in a store without price tags. While you may find what you need, you risk running out of funds. Project managers create budgets to avoid such uncertainties. The primary budget source is cost estimates, covering resources, tasks, and equipment required for project delivery, yielding the total budget for project outcomes.

However, there's more to consider. Incorporate contingency reserve funds for deploying risk mitigation strategies into your budget. Include management reserve if approved by the sponsor. Effective project managers refine their budgets by anticipating cost fluctuations, such as increased distribution costs during holidays or product shortages. Regression analysis assesses historical cost data to estimate potential cost changes based on factors like time of year.

For ongoing budget management, create a time-based cost allocation to monitor projected spending over monthly or quarterly intervals, aligning actual expenditures with the plan. Before finalizing your budget, review costs against expected project benefits to ensure value delivery to the business. By following these steps, your budgeting efforts will provide tangible value, avoiding budgetary crises.

Balancing competing budget constraints

As a project manager, being a mediator is among your most challenging roles. Projects often require mediation because stakeholder expectations can clash due to competing constraints. These conflicts often revolve around trade-offs like cost versus quality but can encompass various issues such as deadlines, regulations, budgets, quality policies, scope, stakeholder priorities, and other business initiatives.

While the project sponsor ultimately makes decisions on these conflicts, you can play a crucial role in facilitating solutions. Presenting alternative options to conflicting stakeholders can save time and reduce frustration. For example, in a cost versus quality debate, you can propose using a mix of higher quality and less expensive materials to achieve both goals or creating two product versions with different cost and quality levels.

To streamline the process, seek your sponsor's approval to explore acceptable alternatives and then engage stakeholders to discuss conditions they find agreeable. While the mediator role may seem daunting, stakeholders often welcome it as they need assistance in reaching acceptable solutions. By facilitating this process, you'll appear as a problem-solving hero, if only for a day.

Organizational considerations for your budget

The phrase "when in Rome, do as the Romans do" applies to project budgeting, where practices can differ between organizations. Several factors influence how you should construct your project budget:

1. Capital vs. Operating Costs: Organizations categorize spending as either capital (e.g., buildings, software) or operating (e.g., utilities, wages). The rules for this classification can vary by country and organization, so align your budget accordingly.

2. Team Release Timing: Determine when team members are released from the project. Ensure you capture the time spent by staff members assigned to various project phases.

3. Viability Metrics: Different organizations measure project viability in various ways, such as the time it takes for the project to break even or using metrics like Net Present Value (NPV). Understand how your organization evaluates project success.

4. Funding Allocation: Know how project funds will be earmarked. This may occur through annual budgets, total forecast allocation at the project's start, or quarterly allocations in Agile projects.

Understanding these organizational considerations is essential when developing your project budget, whether you're in Rome or elsewhere.

Selecting data to analyze when building your budget

Managing your budget during a project can be more challenging than anticipated. To ensure accurate budget reports, you must understand data sources and perform necessary analysis. Here are key considerations for accurate budget management:

1. Labor Hours: Labor costs are often significant but can be challenging to track. Finance departments might use accounting months that don't align with calendar months, and individual employee pay rates may not be disclosed. Generic pay rates per pay grade are often used. Sometimes, monthly cost data is delayed. You may need to track hours and costs independently if finance data isn't timely or suitable.

2. Contractor Costs: Handling contractor or consultant costs depends on the type of contract. Time and materials contracts are straightforward, but fixed-cost contracts require agreements on cost application, often using milestone payments or task completion.

3. Overhead Charges: Many organizations apply overhead charges, which recover costs like senior management and facilities. These charges usually apply to hourly labor costs, but different methods are possible. Understanding how overhead applies to your project is crucial for accurate cost reporting.

4. Materials Procurement: When buying project materials, consider the procurement process. Specific purchase agreements are simple, but volume agreements with vendors can be complex. Understand how costs will be distributed to your project. Also, account for the cost of preparing bid packages and reviewing vendor responses when drafting tenders.

Thoroughly reviewing cost data and understanding these aspects will improve budget report accuracy and establish you as a cost-conscious project manager.

The right metrics for budget management

Managing your project budget is like using a GPS for a road trip. You set your destination, but unexpected turns may happen along the way. To stay on track, use metrics to detect and address budget variances. Here are some tips for understanding and managing these variances:

1. Track Project Team Costs: Plan the hours or percentage of time your project team will work. Monitor their actual hours worked to identify variances and ensure you're on target, including your own time as a project manager.

2. Monitor Completed Tasks: Weekly, compare completed tasks to your planned schedule. If you're falling behind, be prepared to adjust labor costs to catch up, an essential part of budget management.

3. Time Purchases: Pay attention to the timing of equipment or supply payments. Deviations from the plan can create apparent budget variances. Explain these timing differences to stakeholders when necessary.

By following these tips, you can minimize unexpected budget adjustments during your project, much like avoiding frequent "Recalculating" moments on a road trip.

Baseline budget performance

Variance occurs when actual spending deviates from your budget or baseline plan. To effectively manage baseline budget performance, follow these key steps:

1. Adjust Mindset: Understand that estimates can be inaccurate, and unforeseen technical issues or team challenges may arise. Embrace the uncertainty that comes with long-term projects and be prepared to adapt.

2. Monitor Team Effort: Recognize that tasks may take longer or shorter than estimated due to various factors. Keep track of work hours, communicate with your team to understand variances, and request additional staff time when necessary.

3. Manage Risks: Review and address the risks identified in your project. Implement risk response actions and associated costs as needed, with management approval. Monitor the status of your risk contingency reserve and reallocate funds if risks do not materialize.

4. Explore Reallocation Opportunities: Identify opportunities to redistribute funds within the project. Consider reallocating resources from lower-priority requirements to more critical ones. Discuss this with your sponsor to obtain authorization.

5. Handle the Unexpected: Be prepared for unexpected challenges, such as resource departures, budget cuts, or supply chain disruptions. Assess the triple constraints (time, scope, cost) and find alternative solutions. Consult with your sponsor and make informed decisions to keep the project on track.

Remember that your reactions and actions in response to challenges greatly impact baseline budget performance and how you are perceived as a project manager.

The earned value approach

Like children asking, "Are we there yet?" during a journey, project sponsors often seek project status updates to stay informed. Earned value analysis helps gauge project progress effectively. It employs three metrics: Planned Value (PV), Earned Value (EV), and Actual Cost (AC). PV is the planned expenditure at a specific project stage, while EV represents the cost of completed tasks. AC reflects the actual cost, which can deviate from the plan. By graphing these metrics, you can assess project health. For instance, if AC surpasses EV by $1,500, you're over budget. Furthermore, if you've achieved $3,000 in EV but planned for $4,000, there's a performance gap.

Budget forecasting

The earned value approach is highly effective for projecting project status, especially during execution. It aids in estimating the total project cost at completion (EAC) and the funds required from the current project point to its conclusion (ETC). To compute these forecasts, we need the cost performance index (CPI), calculated as EV (earned value) divided by AC (actual cost). Now, let's calculate EAC. Divide the initial project budget estimate by the CPI. For instance, if the budget was 100,000 euros with a CPI of 1.2, EAC equals 100,000 / 1.2, resulting in 83,333 euros. However, if the CPI was 0.85, the calculation is 100,000 / 0.85, resulting in 117,647 euros. This indicates whether you're under or over the original estimate. Now, calculate ETC. Subtract EV from the original budget, then divide by CPI. For instance, with EV at 30,000 euros, an original budget of 100,000 euros, and a CPI of 1.2, ETC is (100,000 - 30,000) / 1.2, equaling 58,333 euros. With a CPI of 0.85, ETC is (100,000 - 30,000) / 0.85, resulting in 82,353 euros. Use these formulas to adjust forecasts as the project advances, taking note of any variances from the plan.

Verifying budget results

Budget reporting is akin to auditing your financial statements; it should be done regularly, and accuracy is crucial. Here are key elements to verify before finalizing your budget reports:

1. Align reporting with consistent timeframes to avoid discrepancies due to non-calendar accounting months.

2. Scrutinize all project purchases for unexpected variances, including materials and additional charges like shipping.

3. Double-check costs allocated to your project to eliminate errors.

4. Review contractor invoices meticulously, verifying hours, rates, and timing.

5. Understand any overhead charges, ensuring fair allocation and avoiding double-counting.

6. Be vigilant about management time, as it can sometimes be double-counted when included in overhead.

Tracking cost of quality and change

I aim to avoid unexpected issues while managing projects, which are frequently caused by quality concerns and scope changes. Let's delve into these potential budget-affecting factors.

Quality management is paramount and should constitute a significant portion of your initial project budget. However, as your project progresses, quality-related matters can impact your budget. There are four key quality aspects to consider:

1. Prevention: This involves strategies to prevent defects and should be part of your initial budget, encompassing plans and designs for quality control.

2. Appraisal: This includes activities like inspections, testing, and assessing supplier quality to ensure your products meet requirements.

Two aspects, in particular, can lead to unexpected budget challenges:

1. Internal Failure: These costs emerge when identifying and rectifying defects, including expenses for rework or scrapping unusable items. We often underestimate the cost of addressing internal failures.

2. External Failure: These are costs incurred when your product or service reaches the customer, including handling complaints, returns, warranty expenses, repairs, and reputation damage recovery. Internal and external failures necessitate project and budget adjustments.

This brings us to the cost of change. Project changes, such as adding or removing tasks due to internal or external failures, require budget updates once you understand the necessary expenditures.

Scope changes can also impact your budget, stemming from new ideas or business requirements. Analyzing the costs associated with these changes is essential for budget integrity. Stakeholder change requests, while beneficial, require budget allocations for management, development, and testing.

Moreover, changes can introduce complexity, especially when they involve technical interfaces, multiple departments, or intricate business processes. Consider estimating the costs associated with increased complexity.

Keep these factors related to quality and scope changes in mind to prevent unexpected surprises in your project, akin to a haunted house full of frights.

Budget information sharing

The saying, "Executives don't read," is often heard, even from my own experience as an executive. It's not entirely true, but it's not far off. Managing a team of over 450 people meant I received around 300 emails daily, making it impossible to read every word and attachment. From many perspectives, it appeared as if I didn't read. However, every executive is deeply interested in the financial status of their area of responsibility.

As project managers, we have tools to generate financial reports, and we want to ensure they are not overlooked. PMI recommends using concise charts, called information radiators, to swiftly convey budget status. Here are some recommended charts:

1. Spending Over Time: This chart compares your actual spending (orange line) to your planned spending (blue line) over time. If the orange line is below the blue line, you've spent less than planned (Example 1). If it's above, you've spent more (Example 2). Adding a one-line explanation of your budget status is crucial because spending more than planned isn't necessarily negative; it could indicate completing more tasks than anticipated. This chart is suitable for agile projects.

2. Earned Value: If you have timely data, consider using Earned Value charts. They plot earned value (EV) and actual costs (AC) on a single chart. If EV exceeds AC, you're on track. If AC is higher, you've overspent on completed tasks.

3. Cost to Address Risk: This chart, similar to Spending Over Time, tracks costs for addressing project risks, including contingency reserve funds. It can also include funding from management reserves and the contingency budget.

While these charts are effective, detailed cost reports by task and purchase are essential because you never know when an executive might decide to delve into the details.

Your budget management toolkit

We've covered various methods for creating and refining your budget and discussed strategies for proactive cost management in your projects. By applying these techniques, you'll have a well-rounded set of tools for handling the financial aspects of project management. However, expanding your finance knowledge can be highly beneficial. Here are some valuable resources to enhance your budget management toolkit:

1. "Simply Finance: An Essential Guide to Finance for Non-Financial Managers" by Susan Hansen: This comprehensive and reader-friendly book delves into accounting practices, offers extensive guidance on budgeting, risk evaluation, and financial decision-making.

2. "The Standard for Earned Value Management" by the Project Management Institute (2020): For a deeper understanding of Earned Value Management, this publication provides detailed insights into using earned value to improve your cost management and forecasting capabilities.

3. Practice Standard for Work Breakdown Structures by the Project Management Institute: If you want to explore work breakdown structures further, this practice standard offers industry-applicable guidelines.

The fundamental goal of project management is to deliver value to the business. By practicing sound budget management and focusing on the benefits your projects bring to your organization, you'll enhance your financial skills and your reputation as a project manager.

Chapter 6 Project Management Teams

Myers-Briggs Type Indicator for project teams

The Myers-Briggs Type Indicator (MBTI) is a well-known tool for understanding how people approach problem-solving, decision-making, and interpersonal interactions. It categorizes individuals into four pairs of traits: introversion/extraversion, sensing/intuition, thinking/feeling, and judging/perception. Each person leans toward one side of each trait, resulting in 16 possible personality types. For instance, an introverted person who prefers sensing, thinking, and judging is classified as ISTJ, known for being responsible and hardworking.

It's essential to note that these traits exist on a scale, allowing for variations in intensity. People can also change over time and in different circumstances. Many resources, including websites and books, offer information and assessments related to MBTI. Exploring this tool can help you better understand your personality and enhance collaboration within your teams.

The DiSC personality profile

The DiSC personality profile is based on four primary personality types, and an individual's behavior is influenced by the strengths of these types. Various companies have created their versions of the DiSC assessment, although they are based on the same personality types. The first type is "D," representing dominant, driver, or doer personalities. They are confident, risk-takers, focused on results, innovative, and organized but can also be argumentative and prone to overcommitting. The next category is "I," standing for inducement, influencers, inspiring, or interactive personalities. They are trusting, talkative, and optimistic, great motivators, and problem solvers but may prioritize popularity over results.

Then there are "S" personalities, which can represent submissive, steady, supportive, or stable traits. They are good listeners, predictable, friendly, and loyal but may resist change and struggle with prioritization. Lastly, "C" stands for compliant or conscientious personalities. They are precise, analytical, and detail-oriented, seeking accuracy through evidence and testing. However, they may become bogged down in details and tend to give in rather than argue.

Within DiSC profiles, there are varying degrees of intensity. The dominant letter typically emerges under pressure, but individuals can exhibit strength in more than one area under different circumstances. For example, someone strong in both "D" and "I" might appear authoritarian during a deadline-driven situation but persuasive and engaging otherwise. Many websites offer DiSC assessments, some of which are free. You can also become certified to administer and use the

DiSC assessment as a trainer or coach to understand and assess your communication and interaction styles more effectively.

Work style assessment

We all have different work styles when it comes to the tasks we prefer and how we approach them. Carson Tate has devised a popular method categorizing individuals into four work style preferences.

1. Prioritizers are logical, analytical, data-driven, and often ask "what" questions.

2. Planners are organized, detail-oriented, follow specific sequences, and ask "how" questions to understand processes.

3. Arrangers are expressive, emotional, supportive, and focus on inclusivity, asking "who" questions about involvement and roles.

4. Visualizers are creative big-picture thinkers who connect complex ideas, often asking "why" questions to understand how things fit together.

Knowing someone's work style helps anticipate their questions and improves communication. It also aids in recognizing potential conflicts within a team, like planners and visualizers collaborating. Understanding work styles can enhance team performance.

StrengthsFinder assessment

Have you ever noticed that you excel at certain tasks at work, tasks that come naturally to you? Don Clifton conducted research and identified 34 themes representing people's personal styles, suggesting that happiness and success at work stem from leveraging one's innate strengths. Clifton categorizes these themes into four domains: strategic thinking, relationship building, influencing, and executing, each containing eight or nine specific strengths.

Understanding your strengths can also shed light on your weaknesses or blind spots. For instance, someone with the "achiever" theme in the executing domain is highly focused on productivity but may struggle with contentment, constantly seeking to do more.

Once you recognize your strengths, it becomes easier to align your work and career with what you excel at and enjoy. Identifying blind spots allows you to compensate for them. As a project manager, you can use CliftonStrengths to help team members understand each other and collaborate more effectively. Explore the CliftonStrengths website or read "Strengths Finder" for deeper insights into yourself and how to enhance your team's success and satisfaction.

Emotional intelligence for project teams

When we hear about someone having a high IQ, we usually associate it with cognitive abilities like math or vocabulary skills. However, when it comes to interacting with people, emotional intelligence (EQ) plays a crucial role. EQ involves recognizing and managing our emotions and understanding and influencing the emotions of others. Daniel Goleman, an authority on emotional intelligence, breaks it down into four main elements:

1. Self-awareness: Knowing oneself, identifying strengths, weaknesses, and personal values.

2. Self-regulation: Controlling emotional responses, avoiding negative or destructive reactions.

3. Social awareness: Including empathy, understanding others' emotions and reasons behind them.

4. Relationship management: Building and maintaining healthy relationships with others.

While intelligence is undoubtedly valuable, especially in technical roles, evidence suggests that emotional intelligence is the most significant predictor of career success. As you climb the corporate ladder, EQ becomes increasingly important. For project managers, EQ is crucial as emotions and relationship dynamics are integral when leading teams.

Tuckman Team-Development Model

Have you ever been part of an outstanding team? What made it exceptional? Were you a great team from the start, or did it take time to learn to work together? Every time we assemble people to work on a project, we're essentially creating a new team. However, being on a team doesn't automatically mean everyone is collaborating effectively. The Tuckman model outlines four phases that groups go through on their path to becoming a cohesive team.

1. Forming: In this initial phase, the group is established, and members are getting to know each other. People tend to be polite and somewhat reserved, unsure of what to expect from others.

2. Storming: As the team works together, friction and conflicts emerge. Differences in approaches or personalities may lead to disagreements and tension.

3. Norming: During this phase, the team addresses issues causing conflicts and establishes rules or norms. This allows for constructive expression of concerns and requires listening and compromise.

4. Performing: With effective communication, conflict resolution, and shared norms, the team is ready to perform efficiently and effectively.

These stages are a natural part of team development. Being prepared for them can help you manage the process. For instance, initiating team-building task at the project's outset can expedite the forming, storming, and norming phases in a low-risk environment. While we all desire high-performing teams, they don't magically appear; they evolve. You can guide them on this journey using the Tuckman model as your framework.

Situational project leadership

Project managers must comprehend various leadership styles and know when to apply them. In the 1960s, Ken Blanchard and Paul Hersey introduced the concept of situational leadership, which combines task and relationship behaviors within leadership styles.

- Task behaviors are work-oriented, like teaching someone how to do their job.

- Relationship behaviors focus on making people feel valued and supported, such as seeking their opinions or offering compliments.

Situational leadership aligns these behaviors with an employee's competence and motivation. Imagine a path through four quadrants:

1. Directive: For employees new to a job with high enthusiasm but low competence, leaders should be directive, emphasizing task guidance.

2. Coaching: As competence grows, and enthusiasm dips, leaders should take a coaching approach, providing clear directions while building relationships.

3. Supporting: With increasing competence and varying commitment, leaders should prioritize relationship-building and reduce task guidance.

4. Delegating: When employees have high competence and engagement, leaders should adopt a delegating style, ensuring understanding and giving autonomy.

Situational leadership helps adapt your leadership style to your team's needs and assists leaders in providing appropriate guidance and support. Being versatile in leadership enhances your effectiveness as a project manager.

Project change and transition management

Projects involve implementing changes within a business, and while change management is emphasized, William Bridges introduced a unique perspective. He distinguished between the work itself and how people respond and adapt to it, referring to this as the transition. This transition consists of three phases:

1. Ending or Letting Go: Dealing with the loss of the old way of doing things.

2. Neutral Zone: A period of uncertainty, often marked by feeling lost and confused.

3. New Beginning: Acceptance of the changes and readiness to move forward.

These phases apply to various life changes, like changing jobs or relocating. Project managers can prepare for these phases by including relevant activities in project plans. For instance, early communication helps stakeholders let go, clear points of contact during the project assist during the neutral zone, and a celebration marks the new beginning. By using the Bridges model, project managers ensure stakeholder engagement throughout the change implementation process.

The Five Dysfunctions of a Team

Have you ever been on a dysfunctional team where decisions were hard to agree on, and morale was low? These situations are common and are addressed by the Lencioni model, a valuable framework for project managers. Patrick Lencioni identifies five dysfunctions that hinder team cohesion:

1. Lack of Trust: Trust is essential for effective teamwork, requiring honesty and transparency.

2. Fear of Conflict: Avoiding conflicts can lead to poor decisions within the team.

3. Absence of Commitment: Without commitment, team members fail to fulfill their responsibilities.

4. Avoidance of Accountability: Shifting blame and evading responsibility impede progress.

5. Inattention to Results: Neglecting to execute tasks well or ignoring necessary improvements.

In contrast, high-performing teams exhibit trust, embrace constructive conflict, demonstrate commitment, accept accountability, and prioritize results. Lencioni's book, "The Five Dysfunctions of a Team," offers further insights on overcoming these challenges. As a project manager, understanding and addressing these dysfunctions can greatly enhance your success in managing project teams.

Manage projects in matrix organizations

Traditionally, businesses have been organized in a hierarchical structure, where each function operates independently, resulting in communication silos. However, this approach is slow and inflexible. Modern businesses are shifting toward matrix structures, where employees work within their functions but are also assigned to cross-functional projects, potentially having multiple supervisors. Matrix structures improve communication and collaboration. There are three types of matrix organizations:

1. Weak Matrix: Functional bosses retain control over performance reviews and promotions.

2. Strong Matrix: Project managers make performance and promotion decisions, while employees remain part of their functional group.

3. Balanced Matrix: Decisions are shared equally between functional and project managers.

Each type has its advantages and disadvantages. The matrix structure significantly affects employee motivation and team dynamics. Understanding the type of matrix in your organization can help you address challenges arising from multiple supervisors effectively.

Managing project teams

As project managers, our success depends on motivating and effectively managing our teams. This book introduced ten common business tools that can aid in this endeavor. Depending on your company's culture, some tools may already be in use, or you can choose the most valuable ones for your needs. Consider checking with your Human Resources department for additional resources. Learning about personality and team management tools serves three purposes: understanding yourself better, comprehending colleagues, and helping others understand themselves and each other. Remember, project managers play a crucial role in helping businesses adapt and thrive.

Chapter 7 Project Management Communication

Project communication

Project managers must understand their project's audience to effectively communicate. Your project has an audience, and even though they're not applauding, they're interested and listening. Tailoring your communication to your audience is essential. Consider this in your everyday life; you share different information with a friend, supervisor, doctor, or stranger on a train. Similarly, your projects have different groups of people to consider: stakeholders, supporters, and spectators.

1. Stakeholders: These are individuals with a vested interest in your project, including upper management, team members, vendors, and customers.

2. Supporters: They assist your project but don't work directly on it. This group includes finance, IT support, facilities, lawyers, and quality assurance.

3. Spectators: These people have an indirect interest in your project, like project managers from other departments.

Your communication plan should address the needs of each group, specifying how to communicate (one-to-one, group meetings, email lists, or reports) and the required information. Create an audience list with these three groups and their respective roles (avoid specifying individuals) to ensure effective project communication without complexity.

Plan the communication

Communication in a project is like a submarine surfacing periodically. Initially, there's a flurry of communication between project managers, directors, stakeholders, and teams. Then, the team works beneath the surface with minimal contact with stakeholders. The project surfaces periodically to update everyone, then submerges again. Stakeholders' communication preferences vary; some want frequent updates, while others prefer none until completion. Therefore, having a project communication plan is crucial.

There are two types of communication plans: stakeholder and event. The stakeholder communication plan focuses on "who" will receive communication and "how" it will be delivered. The event communication plan details meetings, reports, and email blasts, emphasizing the "how."

Start with a stakeholder register if available; if not, create a list. The stakeholder communication plan should address four key aspects:

1. Recipient: Identify who receives the communication.

2. Delivery Method: Specify how it will be delivered (e.g., email, text).

3. Content: Describe what the communication will convey.

4. Timing: Define when they will receive it.

For example, a school superintendent preferred text messages for brief project updates on Fridays after 4:00 p.m. Incorporate stakeholder feedback and keep the plan updated throughout the project.

Encoding and decoding messages

At its core, communication involves encoding and decoding meaning in messages, which can be done through spoken words, writing, gestures, or visuals. However, misunderstandings can occur due to noise in the process. Consider the example of a man yelling "pig" when encountering a pig in the road. His intended meaning might have been "there's a pig, watch out," but the word "pig" can have multiple interpretations.

As a project manager, it's essential to ensure that your messages aren't overshadowed by noise, as excessive noise can lead to miscommunication. You can assess the potential for noise by examining message content, circumstances, and context. Noise can arise from ambiguous words or gestures, the circumstances in which the message is received (e.g., sarcasm in a lengthy meeting), or the context (e.g., a formal business meeting versus a casual encounter).

By recognizing these sources of noise, you can better understand the intended meaning of messages and reduce the chances of miscommunication. Always assume that some level of noise exists in communication to enhance comprehension.

One-way communication

A few years ago, pirates hijacked an Italian cargo ship, the Montecristo. The crew, held captive, secretly placed their ship's location in a bottle and tossed it overboard. NATO ships found the bottle, read the note, and knew the crew was safe. The pirates gave up, and no one was harmed. One-way communication played a crucial role in this incident. While your projects may not involve pirates, you will encounter one-way communication frequently. Most of your project communication is one-way, meaning messages are sent without immediate back-and-forth interaction. Email is a classic example of one-way communication, where messages are pushed into your inbox, often serving as announcements.

However, it's essential to recognize the limitations of one-way communication. It lacks facial expressions and tone of voice, making it less effective for conveying emotions and nuances. Therefore, reserve one-way communication for straightforward, low-emotion messages, such as notifications like "Functional Review Board Meeting Canceled." Avoid using it for sensitive or emotional topics where clarity and understanding are critical.

Behavioral science suggests that interpreting emotions in text can be misleading, as we rely heavily on tone and facial expressions for accurate understanding. Misinterpretations can lead to emotional noise in messages. As a project manager, always follow up on questions arising from one-way messages with a two-way conversation, as questions indicate potential misunderstandings. When choosing between one-way and two-way communication, consider the nature of your message. For sensitive matters, opt for two-way communication, while simple notifications can be conveyed through email or reports.

Two-way communication

In the late 19th century, the invention of the telephone revolutionized communication. Before that, messages had to be transmitted as beeps and then converted into written letters. The telephone introduced the marvel of two-way communication, enabling real-time exchanges through means like face-to-face conversations, phone calls, or instant messaging. As a project manager, two-way communication is a potent tool you should prioritize for essential interactions.

Two-way communication involves real-time conversations, fostering a back-and-forth dialogue between sender and receiver. Face-to-face discussions offer the most effective form of two-way communication due to the advantage of visual cues and body language. Neglecting two-way communication can lead to communication overload, as seen in an organization that discouraged it, resulting in projects bogged down by email exchanges and difficulties obtaining answers.

While one-way communication is more convenient and less time-consuming, it should primarily be reserved for notifications, explanations, and responses to questions. For messages with strong emotional content, two-way communication is essential. Embrace two-way communication as an investment in your project, as it ultimately reduces miscommunication and streamlines communication efforts.

To maximize the benefits of two-way communication, follow these best practices: prioritize listening, avoid multitasking during conversations, address physical barriers that hinder effective communication (e.g., desks as barriers), and be vigilant about distinguishing between desired and actual messages, particularly when receiving good news. Embracing and mastering two-way communication can significantly resolve many communication challenges and enhance your project management effectiveness.

Active listening

Consider the last time you heard a sales announcement in a store; after a few minutes, it becomes background noise. This can also happen with your project when too many messages are sent. Project managers have various ways to deliver messages, but effective communication involves active listening, which includes rinsing, remixing, and rewording.

Rinsing means discerning relevant from irrelevant content in messages. This step involves eliminating anything unrelated or overly technical that could obscure the core issue.

Remixing and rewording occur when you synthesize what someone says and paraphrase it back to them. For instance, if an engineer raises multiple points about a data migration project but only needs to reschedule, focus on that specific request.

Maintain discipline in active listening to avoid getting sidetracked by irrelevant details. After rinsing the information, remix it to make it clear to both parties. For example, if the engineer doesn't explicitly request a reschedule but mentions coaching his son's baseball team, clarify his intent by asking, "Are you asking me to postpone the test migration to another weekend?" Repeat the rinsed and remixed information as needed to ensure an accurate understanding and facilitate a more informed response.

Formal communication

In your career, appearing professional matters, just like wearing a suit and tie can command attention. Communication can also be formal or informal. Formal messages exude professionalism, much like dressing up in a suit and tie. Examples of formal communication include standard office memos and slide presentations.

Formal communication carries specific assumptions and sets expectations for the recipient's response. The choice between formal and informal communication depends on both the audience and the message's content. For instance, formal communication is suitable when updating a supervisor, while an email may suffice for external contacts.

Consider two aspects when deciding on formal communication: the audience and the message itself. Consequential messages should generally use formal communication, which can be delivered in written or verbal forms.

Formal written communication, like negotiating a contract, is essential for certain situations. On the other hand, formal verbal communication, such as a slide presentation, demonstrates the importance and professionalism of the message. Adjust your communication style based on your audience, like presenting formally for project stakeholders but using informal communication for a new hire.

Remember that formal communication conveys professionalism and seriousness, suitable for specific messages.

Informal communication

While formal communication receives significant attention in project management, a substantial portion of your communication is informal, which can be categorized as informal written and informal verbal communication. Informal communication encompasses all unprepared forms of communication. Email is a prevalent medium for informal written messages, often casually presented. Informal messages are typically brief and include notices, such as meeting cancellations or updates.

Informal verbal communication, although less common than email, plays a significant role in your daily interactions. These discussions occur in cubicles or provide feedback following formal meetings. Informal communication allows for more straightforward inquiries and a less formal atmosphere, making it easier to obtain unfiltered information.

For instance, during formal presentations, it may be impolite to correct errors immediately, but informal chats afterward can clarify misunderstandings. To facilitate informal communication, project managers can stand near their teams, adopt "management by walking around" (MBWA), and ensure accessibility for stakeholders.

It's crucial to maintain a friendly and problem-solving demeanor to encourage informal chats. Neglecting these interactions and relying solely on formal reports can leave you partially unaware of important information.

Categorize the stakeholders

As a project manager, you'll encounter various individuals interested in your project, particularly stakeholders, who perceive that the project affects them in some way, whether real or perceived. Your communication plan includes a stakeholder register, listing everyone with a stake in the project. For larger projects, you'll develop a stakeholder management plan that builds upon this register.

The initial step in the stakeholder management plan is categorizing stakeholders not as individuals but by their roles. For instance, roles like "lead doctor" or "insurance partner" are preferred over specific names or company designations. This role-based categorization streamlines communication by identifying common needs among stakeholders sharing a role.

To further refine your approach, use the P3I technique to classify stakeholders based on their Power, Impact, Interest, and Influence. Power relates to an individual's ability to influence decisions within the organization, often observed in executive management roles. Impact pertains to the resources provided to influential stakeholders, even if they lack direct power. Interest levels in the project can vary, with some stakeholders showing little interest despite their power. Influence reflects the stakeholders you collaborate closely with during the project.

Applying the P3I technique to categorize stakeholders enhances the utility of your register and informs your stakeholder management plan.

Prioritize the stakeholders

As a project manager, time is of the essence, and you'll often receive requests for swift communication. To manage this, use a Power and Interest grid, which is solely for your use and not to be shared with stakeholders. It helps you prioritize your communication effectively.

The Power and Interest grid consists of four quadrants, starting from the top left and moving clockwise:

1. High-Power, Low-Interest Stakeholders: These are top-priority stakeholders requiring minimal communication to keep them informed. Label them as "Keep Satisfied" in your Stakeholder Register.

2. High-Power, High-Interest Stakeholders: Manage their communication closely, providing comprehensive project information. Use "Manage Closely" in your register for this group.

3. Low-Power, High-Interest Stakeholders: Keep them informed through one-way communication, and label them as "Inform" in your register.

4. Low-Power, Low-Interest Stakeholders: Monitor them to ensure they don't become higher priority. Label them as "Monitor" in your register.

Incorporate these priority labels into your Stakeholder Register, specifically in a "Priority" column. This system will guide your communication strategy and can be included in your overall communication management plan within your project management plan.

Manage executive stakeholders

I once worked on a project where the executive sponsor regularly interacted with the team. However, there was a communication gap between the executive and the developers. The developers tended to highlight their daily challenges, which made it seem like they were overwhelmed to the executive. Executives have their own way of speaking and might not be accustomed to hearing such challenges in detail. Communicating with executives poses a unique challenge, as you must not only monitor their communications but also use language that resonates with them.

When communicating with executives, consider the following:

1. Understand Their Key Motivators: Executives are primarily concerned with successful project delivery, which differs slightly from a project manager's focus on timing and budget. Tailor your communication to emphasize quality and delivery. Highlight recent achievements and reassure them about the project's progress. If there are delays, communicate through formal written channels.

2. Be Concise: Executives appreciate concise updates. Avoid presenting a list of unresolved challenges without recommended solutions, as it may give the impression that you're not effectively managing the project. Provide a brief, high-level summary of your project's status, akin to an elevator pitch.

3. Grasp the Big Picture: Understand where your project fits within the executive's broader portfolio. Executives face challenges beyond your project, so consider how your project aligns with the organization's overall goals. Show that you have a holistic view of the organization, not just a narrow focus on your project.

Incorporate these principles into your communication with executives to ensure effective interaction and a better understanding of your project's progress in the larger context.

Answer tough questions

As a project manager, you'll inevitably face tough questions from stakeholders. It's natural to want to soften the answer or avoid the question, but it's essential to resist these instincts. Let me share a story from when I worked on a school project. We were behind schedule, and a stakeholder confronted me with, "Why should we fund this project if the software isn't working?" In such situations, remember the acronym NIECE: Never get upset, Illustrate with examples, Empathize, Clarify the question, and Explain your answer.

In my case, I didn't get defensive, but instead, I asked for specific examples. The stakeholder mentioned an issue with creating student accounts during a demonstration. Using active listening, I sought clarification to understand precisely which part of the software was problematic. I focused on understanding the question rather than confronting the stakeholder.

Empathy is crucial throughout this process. Acknowledge any mistakes or shortcomings and understand the stakeholder's perspective. Once you've clarified the original question, you'll have a clearer understanding of what the stakeholder is truly concerned about.

The most important part of the NIECE approach is explaining your answer. Stakeholders often seek answers they can use elsewhere. Provide a comprehensive response, outlining your thought process and rationale. For example, you might say, "I believe we shouldn't cancel the project because we opted for rapid development due to expected customer changes. However, this approach may lead to more debugging time." After explaining your answer, consider offering suggestions to enhance the process.

In my case, the stakeholder decided not to cancel the project and even used my explanations to address concerns with other schools. Prioritizing a focused response to the question significantly improved our communication.

Cross-functional communication

When working in a large organization, you may encounter the challenge of communicating within cross-functional teams. These teams consist of employees from various functional areas collaborating to achieve a common goal. Functional areas can include sales, finance, marketing, human resources, and technology, resulting in individuals from diverse backgrounds coming together on a single team.

The primary challenge in cross-functional teams is the assumption of shared language and concepts among team members from different functional areas. Sales professionals might naturally discuss quarterly sales goals and conversion rates, but these terms may be unfamiliar to software developers. To address this challenge effectively, it's essential to prioritize cross-training among team members from different functional areas.

While it may seem tedious for software developers to grasp sales terminology and vice versa, this shared language is fundamental to the team's efficiency. It allows for smoother communication, quicker decision-making, and an equitable playing field where everyone can contribute to discussions without needing to clarify jargon constantly.

For example, in an organization I worked for, a cross-functional team focused on a finance product. Finance experts explained concepts like cash flow, assets, and liabilities to developers, while software developers clarified JavaScript, mobile apps, and test-driven development. This shared language expedited decision-making and fostered a sense of inclusivity, as team members no longer wasted time on terminology clarification.

In cross-functional teams, both teaching and learning are crucial. Don't hesitate to ask questions when you encounter unfamiliar terms or concepts. Simultaneously, be patient when explaining concepts from your own functional area to others who may be unfamiliar. Patience is essential when conveying complex ideas in simple terms, and you might even gain insights during the process.

To facilitate communication further, consider creating a shared jargon board, listing acronyms and industry-specific terms. Some teams may benefit from brief training sessions where team members educate their peers about key concepts from their respective functional areas. These efforts contribute to establishing a shared language and fostering smoother communication within cross-functional teams.

Why we meet

Meetings often go by various names like briefings, innovation circles, or executive overviews, but many of them are essentially standard conference meetings. There are three primary types of meetings: conference meetings, work group meetings, and brainstorming meetings.

1. Conference Meetings: These are typical office meetings with one person presenting slides on a specific topic to a group of five or more participants. They are common in most organizations and are used to align everyone or share information. However, they are often considered inefficient and have changed little over time. They serve a social function, helping build networks, establishing one's place in the organization, and facilitating interactions with colleagues you might not otherwise meet.

2. Work Group Meetings: Designed to solve specific problems, work group meetings involve a maximum of five participants. These meetings are focused and collaborative, addressing issues like system malfunctions or employee performance.

3. Brainstorming Meetings: These meetings are more complex to organize, with a maximum of seven participants. They aim to generate new ideas and require skilled facilitation. Participants bounce ideas off each other, fostering creativity and innovation.

It's important for meeting organizers to understand these differences and select the most suitable type of meeting for their purpose. Additionally, naming the meeting appropriately helps communicate the agenda effectively.

Meeting management

As a meeting organizer, your goal is to ensure that meetings have a clear purpose. Utilize the SHARKS approach for efficient meetings:

- S: Start by stating the agenda at the beginning of the meeting. Be explicit about why everyone is there.

- H: Beware of hijackers who might derail the meeting with unrelated topics. Politely redirect discussions back to the agenda.

- A: Encourage participants to add relevant information. Avoid merely agreeing with others, as it can be distracting.

- R: Repeat the agenda at the end of the meeting and assess what was achieved compared to the agenda.

- K: Keep meetings small and concise. Continuously review and refine the list of attendees to include only those necessary.

- S: Schedule future meetings outside of the current meeting. Use email for scheduling to respect participants' time.

Following the SHARKS approach helps you establish a reputation for running productive meetings, where participants are well-prepared and focused on achieving goals.

Decide what to include

Purple prose, a term rooted in ancient Rome, refers to overly elaborate and wordy language used to cover up weak ideas. Today, it's still prevalent in reports, where some believe it makes ideas seem more thoughtful. However, reports should prioritize brevity and clarity. Here are tips to avoid purple prose:

1. Use minimal language: Avoid wordy phrases like "utilize" or "prioritize" when simpler terms suffice.

2. Prefer active voice: Instead of passive voice that lacks ownership, use active voice to convey ideas more clearly.

3. Embrace bullet points: Utilize bullet points for succinct communication, as they are effective for busy stakeholders and can be instrumental in project funding decisions.

Clear language

Clear and effective writing is a valuable skill, though not everyone possesses it naturally. Rather than trying to imitate rare individuals who effortlessly write well, focus on developing your own writing abilities. Complex writing doesn't necessarily make your ideas more impressive; simplifying complex concepts is the real challenge in effective communication. Here's a three-step approach to improve your writing:

1. Spit: Start by freely expressing your thoughts without worrying about grammar or punctuation. Write everything that comes to mind in a document. This serves as a foundation for your writing.

2. Polish: After an initial draft, step away from your document to gain a fresh perspective. During this phase, refine your writing by rearranging paragraphs for better flow and clarity. Consider your audience and their knowledge level as you revise.

3. Shine: After another break, review your document once more. Look for and eliminate unnecessary restatements and extra material to make your writing concise and polished.

By following this approach, you can become a clearer and more efficient writer without getting stuck staring at a blank page. Remember, the first step is getting your ideas down on paper.

Simple charts

Simple sketches are potent tools for conveying complex ideas, enhancing the clarity of your reports for all readers, including those who think visually. These sketches can be charts, graphs, or basic figures, like a smiley face to indicate a positive outcome, a bar chart for comparisons, or a light bulb to symbolize an idea.

Sketched visuals leverage context to convey ideas without the need for additional explanations. For instance, a smiley face above a dollar bill conveys increased profits intuitively. Sketches are particularly effective for illustrating relative differences, displaying relationships, and sparking discussions.

Incorporating eye-catching sketches can also capture and hold your readers' attention, making your reports more engaging. Try adding colorful charts to your reports and observe how team members tend to focus on these visuals amidst lengthy text. These simple sketches provide a brief but impactful way to enhance communication in your reports.

Next steps

For those preparing for the Project Management Professional Exam, mastering the terminology used by the Project Management Institute (PMI) is crucial. This book has covered much of the PMI's communication management knowledge area, providing a solid grasp of the fundamental concepts.

As a project manager, communication is a primary focus, and there are always opportunities for improvement. Never stop refining your communication skills, as effective communication is highly rewarding and an invaluable asset to your career in project management.

Printed in Great Britain
by Amazon

40041806R00069